Early Praise for *What's a*

"In our current interconnected and interdependent work environment, all teammates need to feel supported, encouraged and valued to go higher together. This is equally true for how men and women work together, both laterally and vertically. With *What's a Guy to Do?* Jennifer Crittenden addresses these very real and very sensitive topics in a candid and easily understood manner that will also have you laughing out loud even if you might recognize yourself in a description or two. If learning to work better with women is your goal, this book is your answer."

> ~ Keith Ferrazzi, author of the #1 NY Times Bestseller
> *Who's Got Your Back* and *Never Eat Alone*

"A practical, enjoyable, and easy-to-read guide to a sometimes confusing and rapidly-changing environment. Filled with plain-spoken examples for how people should treat each other—naturally, respectfully, and focused, irrespective of gender or other irrelevant traits. The author challenges all of us by providing a balanced, realistic, and even humorous approach to a serious subject. Jennifer shows us all how to be more trusting, more respectful, and more productive by doing the right thing."

> ~ Daniel J. Adams, Senior Vice President,
> Business Banking, Wells Fargo Bank

"It took me nearly 40 years to learn and put into practice what Jennifer has artfully condensed into these few pages. I remember walking in to one of my first jobs in the early '80s and seeing a banner above a desk saying 'Sexual harassment will not be reported, but it will be graded.' A lot has changed since then… and a lot has not. Open mockery and harassment may be taboo; however, it is extremely clear from the #MeToo movement that the bad behavior is hiding behind a thin veil of political correctness—or an office door. *What's a Guy To Do?* provides anyone with a trove of tools to tear down biases in our workplaces. This is a must read."

> ~ Todd C. Williams, President,
> eCameron, Inc.

What's a Guy to Do?

How to Work with Women

Jennifer K. Crittenden

WHISTLING
RABBIT
PRESS

San Diego, California

Contact the publisher at info@whistlingrabbitpress.com.

Contact the author, Jennifer K. Crittenden, at her website discreetguide.com.

Cover design by Victoria Davies at VC Book Cover Designs
Interior design by Arc Manor Book Design

Paperback ISBN: 978-0-9847360-3-4
eBook ISBN: 978-0-9847360-7-2

Publisher's Cataloging-in-Publication data

Names: Crittenden, Jennifer K., author.
Title: What's a guy to do? : how to work with women / Jennifer K. Crittenden.
Description: Includes index. | San Diego, CA: Whistling Rabbit Press, 2018.
Identifiers: ISBN 978-0-9847360-3-4 (pbk.) | 978-0-9847360-7-2 (ebook) | LCCN 2018905941
Subjects: LCSH Women employees. | Women in the professions--United States. | Women--Employment. | Work--Social aspects. | Sex role in the work environment. | Sex differences (Psychology) | Sex discrimination. | Sexual harassment of women. | Communication in organizations. | Men--Attitudes. | Women--Attitudes. | Interpersonal relations. | Organizational behavior. | Corporate culture. | Businessmen. | Businesswomen. | BISAC BUSINESS & ECONOMICS / Workplace Culture
Classification: LCC HD6060.6 .C75 2018 | DDC 650.1--dc23

Published by
Whistling Rabbit Press
San Diego, California
whistlingrabbitpress.com

To the good guys

Also by Jennifer K. Crittenden

The Discreet Guide for Executive Women: How to Work Well with Men (and Other Difficulties), San Diego: Whistling Rabbit Press, 2012

You, Not I: Exceptional Presence through the Eyes of Others, San Diego: Whistling Rabbit Press, 2014

The Mammoth Letters: Running Away to a Mountain Town, San Diego: Whistling Rabbit Press, 2017

Contents

A Reasonable Man

Every man's reason is his own rightful umpire.
~ Thomas Jefferson

A few years ago, after I gave a talk about workplace gender issues, a guy in the audience asked me how he could signal to his female colleagues that he was on their side. He said they always assumed he was a chauvinist because he was an older white man. I asked him if he was looking for a password or a secret handshake. "Yeah!" he said enthusiastically. I told him to keep on doing the right thing and his co-workers would catch on. The advice felt a little lame at the time. Now it feels really lame. Recently, a new entrepreneur asked me what he could do to make sure that he was developing a company that would be welcoming to women. That time I was prepared with more specifics.

First, let's applaud these guys. They are exceptionally good guys, not just tolerant of women but openly supportive of them. We've been hearing so much about bad guys that we have forgotten how many decent, respectful, well-intentioned men are out there. I'm alarmed that we have fallen into what humor columnist and author Dave Barry called the "national consensus that all men are pond scum with hands."

Next, let's acknowledge that 2017 was a watershed year for recognizing the extent and viciousness of sexual misconduct in the workplace. The women's stories have been truly horrific. When emotions run that high, however, we run the risk of throwing someone to the wolves for a fairly minor infraction. Just as there is a difference between stealing paper clips and embezzling thousands of dollars, so there is between an inappropriate joke and sexual assault. Nevertheless, so much vitriol has been spewed that any reasonable man would be wondering if he really knows what acceptable behavior in the workplace is anymore.

In case you are that man, this book is intended to simplify a complicated topic and provide you with basic ground rules that will lay a foundation for how to engage productively and positively with your female co-workers. And if you're a guy who suspects or is pretty sure that men have an advantage in the workplace but doesn't know what to do about it, we'll get into that too.

Working comfortably with the opposite sex can offer great rewards. Not only is it more fun, an environment in which employees feel welcome and perform well leads to more successful outcomes. Being surrounded by talented and high-performing individuals is very stimulating. You don't want to miss out on the talent pool offered by half the population.

REAL PROBLEMS

The book is also intended to identify those behaviors that make women uneasy in the workplace. Many of those don't qualify as sexual misconduct, but if we desire a culture in which women can flourish, it's worth addressing them. Not every complaint a woman has about her workplace is valid; but in my twenty-some years of experience in the corporate world and in my subsequent work as a career coach and trainer, I hear enough repetition about certain circumstances that you should hear about them too.

People disagree about what is sexual harassment or even offensive behavior, and arguing about it clouds the seriousness of the problem. When it comes to sexual harassment, we *don't* know it when we see it. According to a Reuters survey conducted in January 2018, respondents split about whether "unwanted compliments about your appearance," "dirty jokes," or "unwanted hugs" constituted sexual harassment. In my view, the wrong question was asked. We shouldn't be worried *only* if these behaviors constitute sexual harassment. According to the legal definition, they probably don't, unless other conditions are met. But are they conducive to a productive workplace? If they are unwanted, they clearly aren't. And that should concern a good manager—and a reasonable man.

We are often surprised when a popular guy is exposed as a harasser. A manipulative operator can be charming and charismatic until he pulls off his mask behind closed doors. That presents a special problem for a woman who suffers at the hands of such an individual because she knows that people will have a hard time believing her story. Organizations are often loath to take action against someone who is well-liked and otherwise a good performer. Bad actors survive in the working world because their sexual misconduct is swept under the rug, and the women are encouraged to drop their complaints.

DO WOMEN REALLY HAVE IT SO BAD?

Many men wonder if women are really playing at a higher difficulty setting. Early in my career, a guy told me (with some hostility) that I would probably do better than he would simply because I was a woman. To his way of thinking, women got special treatment and had advantages that would carry me far beyond him as I sailed to the top of the organization. I tried not to bust out laughing. You can't deny someone else's perception, but even a casual review of the facts makes it obvious that isn't the case for most women. Although . . . maybe being clueless and resentful did hold him back.

That said, do some women have it easier in the workplace? I imagine so. Relatives or lovers of powerful men often are placed in high positions without earning their stripes. Are some companies biased toward women such that women always end up in leadership positions? It seems likely, right? I don't know of any, but they surely exist.

The real question is: What does that mean for you? If you go around with a chip on your shoulder about how lucky women are, it may not help you be successful either. Here's what I would suggest: Ask the women around you. Ask your colleagues if they think your workplace presents a level playing field to women. Ask your wife or girlfriend if she experiences discrimination at her place of employment. Ask your mother what it was like when she was working. If you gather real stories from real women, I think you'll develop a meaningful picture of what women face.

THE BACKLASH

Complaints about sexual harassment sometimes provoke comments like, "Oh, you can't say anything anymore" or "Men and women can't act naturally around each other anymore" or "All this stuff prohibits productivity." I used to hear that kind of nonsense during sexual harassment training. It's a bunch of BS, and most guys recognize real sexual harassment in less than a minute. Coercing a woman into sex in exchange for professional advancement? That ain't hindering productivity. Repeatedly rubbing up against a woman at work? That's not men and women acting naturally around each other, unless you think humans have no more self-control than wild beasts. Discussing a woman's physical attributes in her presence? I'm going to answer that one with a question. Are you an asshat?

I've also heard people say that rules about sexual harassment keep "men from acting like men." That struck me as particularly suspect. It seems to me that a man shouldn't have to humiliate or intimidate a woman to feel like a man. Can't a man be a man anywhere? I'm picturing a man on a mountain top with no women around for miles. Isn't he still a man? Surely, in a workplace with mixed genders, men can still be men. They just don't have to be jerks.

But reasonable guys are different from those slimeballs. And it's fair for them to be asking for straightforward answers in the face of lawsuits, summary firings, and reputations being ruined.

NOT MUCH OUT THERE

When I conceived of this book, I looked around to see what advice was available for men working with women. I found almost nothing. There's an odd article or two for men working in female-dominated departments; one advises you to discuss your feelings with your co-workers. Another from 1943 contains advice for supervisors of women who were hired into men's jobs during WWII. It includes such gems as requiring a doctor's exam to rule out nervous disorders, keeping women busy because they lack initiative but like change, and hiring middle-aged women because young ones are too flirtatious and old ones tend to be cantankerous. Oh, and "husky" ones are more even-tempered and efficient than their underweight sisters. My favorite was "Never ridicule a woman—it breaks her spirit and cuts her efficiency." Maybe they got one thing right. The rest of it felt a *little* dated. Surely, we can do better than that.

WHAT WORKS

This book isn't heavy on political correctness. I've grown impatient with much of what has been recommended following overwhelming evidence of widespread sexual misconduct. I often reject what is suggested by academics or so-called experts because I don't think it would work. Some of the recommended language I hear is so contrived as to be jaw-dropping. If someone talked like that on the manufacturing floor, the guys would laugh their butts off. I've tried instead to explain how to handle situations from a sensitive but practical standpoint. We're trying to get work done after all, and that should be our focus.

USE YOUR HEAD

Because I hear and read the same complaints from women over and over, it is fair to identify the common issues and address them. Some of them might surprise you, and some are fairly predictable. What I do here is point them out and give you some tools to cope with them. I've tried not to whine too much about how unfair it all is (for either sex) and just present the reality as it is. I've tried to keep a sense of humor, and I hope you do too.

I will ask this of you. When I suggest something, consider it and maybe try it out. If it feels wrong for your situation, give it a pass. There's too much mindless conformity in the corporate world as it is. We can make observations about men and women; and, in a book like this, we can try to broaden those specifics into general advice about working with women, but only with caution. The women you encounter might be very different from the ones I've worked with, and figuring them out will require you to use your thinking cap. The dynamics between you and your male and female co-workers are dependent on subtle details of the company culture and the personalities involved. Because I can't cover all eventualities in a small book, you will have to think for yourself and imagine what a reasonable person would do. When guys get into trouble, it's sometimes because they haven't used their brains at all, or have malevolent intentions. Naturally, that's not you.

WHO'S WITH ME?

Six years ago, I wrote a book targeted at women working in male-dominated companies. I was inspired to write it because I was disappointed when many of my female colleagues chose to drop out early in their careers, leaving me behind. Their reasons for doing so were often politically correct (to stay home with the kids, go into consulting, or start their own businesses), but I suspected they were discouraged by their lack of success and by political problems. Some of their difficulty was because they didn't understand how to operate in a male environment, and I wanted to address those gender issues that we often don't talk about so that future women could be more successful. The book was well received, but a friend told me that a colleague had criticized it for being "more of the same," that it's "always about what women have to do, how women have to behave better, how they have to fix themselves."

That's a valid criticism and caused me to adjust my attitude. I firmly believe that we will not make real headway in improving our workplaces without help from male colleagues. We can preach at the women all we want, do this, do that, be more assertive, but not too much, just be perfect, okay? We can coach and train them to behave more like men, or less like them. We can write book after book about how they can succeed. But until the guys get in the game and decide that enough is enough, we're just nibbling at the edges.

ONE DAY AT A TIME

The animosity between the sexes has intensified during the past year, something I find alarming and detrimental to my efforts to improve people's work experiences. I try to address what's in front of me each day to bring about positive change. If you focus on your own situation and your own co-workers to make their lives better, you can have a big impact. Every day, you can be an agent for change, improving your work culture and bringing civility back to the world.

A Word about Women

Men are from Earth, women are from Earth. Deal with it.
~ George Carlin

Defenders of the status quo sometimes announce their bias by proclaiming that men and women are different. Their argument goes something like this: "Men and women are different! We need separate bathrooms!" Or, if the prevalence of sexual harassment comes up, they announce that men and women are different, apparently to justify bad male behavior. I find that argument specious. The more you look at it, the more useless it becomes. Of the differences that can be proven scientifically, none seem to predict anything that would help you interact with women in the workplace.

Then there are the advocates of female mysticism, and they too believe that men and women are different, although in their case, they believe that women are *better*. If you delve into the literature about female leadership, you will discover a common theme about how great women are. According to those believers, women are more sensitive, more intuitive, more collaborative, more empathetic, with higher emotional intelligence than men. Allegedly, we are mystical creatures with untapped capabilities that, if only allowed to flourish, would transform leadership in this country. In my opinion, it's all hooey.

"THE SECRET SAUCE"

Men sometimes talk publicly about how great women are, a different flavor of the "women are magical" thesis. They'll talk about how the women are more considerate than men, better team players, and a pleasure to work with. I've been hearing it more lately from male CEOs when they're speaking in a public forum. It's like political correctness gone mad.

Here's an example. See if it makes you whack yourself on the forehead as it did me. Jack Ma is the CEO of Alibaba Group, one of the world's largest e-commerce businesses. His quotes on women are frequently printed in the press, such as that women are "the secret sauce" of his company and that aspiring companies should hire more women. Here's one head-scratcher: "Men think about themselves more; women think about others more. Women think about taking care of their parents, their children." Okay, guys, good to know that you're a bunch of unfeeling narcissists.

At the World Economic Forum in Davos, Switzerland, in 2018, Ma said that "if you want your company to operate with wisdom, with care, women are the best." And how does Mr. Ma put his money where his mouth is? He is apparently very proud that over 30 percent of his company's leadership is female. Thirty percent. Yeah. I know what you're thinking. And these things get printed without a hint of irony.

Anyway, that's all a bunch of hooey too. You already know that some women are definitely not a pleasure to work with, so don't say stupid stuff about women. A bright woman doesn't want you to put her on a pedestal. She wants to earn your respect on her own merits.

MAYBE NOT THAT DIFFERENT

Various studies say various things, but most conclude that more variation exists among men and among women than between the average man and the average woman. For example, the average man is bigger than the average woman, but the difference between really large men and really small men is much greater than the difference between the averages of the sexes. Which means it's not a very interesting observation for practical purposes. You can't reliably predict how big or small a man or a woman will be, nor any other physical or psychological characteristic. Each person must be considered as an individual. It's harder to do that than make assumptions, but assumptions based on sex can be wrong. Sorry, I know it makes your world more complex (but also more interesting!).

My personal conclusion is that men and women aren't as different as we think. This played out with my own study about executive presence. I developed a self-assessment tool to evaluate people's self-confidence about factors such as public speaking, networking, and approachability. In the data from more than four hundred professionals, I was sure the statisticians would find a significant difference between men's and women's responses. Nope. Both were equally confident (or not) about their presence. That was eye-opening and caused me to reconsider my own biases. You're better off assuming women and men are more alike than you think, until it's been proven otherwise. I hope you find that comforting. It means you're not dealing with alien creatures. Most women you work with will think a lot like you, even if they look different. Also nice to know, dear reader, that you yourself are not defined by your sex.

BUT NOT TREATED THE SAME

An abundance of evidence exists however that, regardless of how alike or different we are, men and women are not treated the same by parents, teachers, peers, or managers. And in the workplace, the sad reality is that a lot of people, both men and women, don't like working with women. They don't hire them, they don't promote them, they don't keep them.

Historically, according to a Gallup poll taken periodically since 1953, both men and women prefer to have a male boss, by a wide margin. What could be the reasons? Perhaps they think male bosses have more power and potential. Perhaps guys are uncomfortable reporting to a female supervisor. And perhaps they've had a female boss who wasn't very good or fair or nice. I know, I know, you're not supposed to say things like that anymore; but, believe it or not, I've seen female bosses out in the wild who were terrible. Uh-oh, I hear the political correctness police at my door.

The poll deserves a footnote: In 2017, for the first time ever, the Gallup poll showed that a majority of Americans showed no preference for one gender over the other. That was one month after accusations about Harvey Weinstein, a former film producer, were made public. So there's that.

A HELPING HAND

I bring all this up so you know up front this book isn't about how great women are, but also so you think about how this larger context can affect a woman working in your midst. You see, she knows that a lot of people don't like working with women. She knows there's a reason that only twenty-three of Fortune 500 companies' CEOs are women. She knows that a lot of people disapprove of working women. She's been told how hard it will be for her to prove herself. She knows these things. *And she's still here*. At least, let's give her that.

The rest of the book is about how you can help her do the best job she can.

Why Bother?

There comes a time when one must take a position that is neither safe, nor politic, nor popular, but he must take it because conscience tells him it is right.
~ Martin Luther King Jr.

I have a grave concern that all that's happened in 2017 will drive men and women further apart and make their interactions at work even more contrived and artificial. When I read contradictory advice for women, when I see the nutty things some women complain about, when consultants make recommendations that would be ineffective and stupid, even I lose patience. I get frustrated when we complicate some simple issues that would really help women in the workplace. When we start fighting over day care, nitpicking statistics, and generally bad-mouthing each other, it's not productive. If I were a guy who had been told that a female candidate sitting across from me needs free child care, that my company will perform better if I hire her but only if I change how I measure good performance, or that other women will object if she gets any special treatment because she is a mother, I would be tempted to spread my arms wide and say, "Why don't you all just go on home now."

Add to this steaming heap the outrage of the past year about sexual misconduct, and we have a real mess. We're already on shaky ground if guys hesitate to hire women because they are too much trouble. If they are further discouraged by potential claims of sexual harassment, we're in a backlash tsunami. Gender discrimination in hiring practices is easy to disguise, and it would be a long time before those lawbreakers were caught. My biggest fear is that men will simply stop hiring women.

ONE EFFECT OF #METOO

In early 2018, the nonprofit organization LeanIn.Org conducted an online poll to assess the #MeToo campaign's effect on male managers. Nearly half said they were now uncomfortable participating in common work activities with a woman, such as working alone, mentoring, or socializing together. Nearly 30 percent said they were uncomfortable working alone with a woman; that's nearly double the previously recorded number. The percentage of men now saying they were uncomfortable mentoring a woman went from 5 to 16 percent. Increasingly, men didn't want to have dinner or travel with a woman. Look, this is really bad news. It's bad news for women. And it's bad news for men.

It's already troubling that in many companies, men "forget" to invite their female colleagues to their before- or after-hours events. Now, men are openly saying that they are uncomfortable being with a woman apparently because they fear a harassment claim. Setting aside for the moment whether the fear is logical or not, that reaction is disastrous for women and for companies who wish to create a workplace in which women can flourish. Let's see if I can convince you—just one guy—of how bad this is.

IT'S NOT JUST BREAKFAST

One morning I was invited to a breakfast meeting at a local deli. When I walked in at 7 a.m., I was thunderstruck. The place was humming; every table was full. People were talking and persuading, pitching and hustling, questioning and selling. And other than me and the waitresses—there were no women. There wasn't even a spouse. When I mentioned this phenomenon to a friend, she said, "Oh, you didn't know? That's where deals are done in this town."

If women aren't invited, they have no access to that kind of power. Women need to be in on deal making if they are to be successful. As we strive toward equality in the workplace, women must have the same opportunities that men do. Just as junior men benefit from socializing with their male bosses, so will women. Women must be just as present to build networks, get to know their colleagues personally, and receive the kind of advice that men provide to other men in an informal context.

I advise my female clients to take advantage of every opportunity to hang out with their male colleagues; that's how you build strong collegial relationships. Men need to get to know women so they will refer them for promotions, board seats, and professional opportunities. If men won't work naturally and comfortably with their female co-workers, the women will miss out on important opportunities for learning and advancement. In my opinion, if that happens, women will never compete on a level playing field.

THE BILLY GRAHAM / MIKE PENCE RULE

You may have heard one of those famous guys announcing that he wouldn't eat alone with a woman who wasn't his wife. I assume it was to avoid an appearance of impropriety, though it would be funnier if it was because he thought he was so hot no woman could keep her hands off him.

Unfortunately, after #MeToo, others started talking the same language. Several pundits suggested that men simply stop meeting with women altogether and that adopting the Graham/Pence Rule would solve those problems. In response, others were obliged to mention the obvious: Prohibiting meetings between men and women isn't practical if people are trying to conduct normal business which requires confidential conversations. Others observed that this reaction would have a punitive element to it, like . . . Complain about men? Fine, no meetings for you!

YELLING AT THE RADIO

During this time, a guy called into a radio show while I was listening to ask if it was still okay to meet with a female subordinate in his office with the door closed. To my rage, the host of the show said he shouldn't do that anymore. I'll spare you my shouting and banging on the steering wheel (perhaps this book was conceived in that precise moment), but, *of course*, it's okay to meet with her in private. My goodness, imagine if you had some important confidential matter to discuss, like you were actually doing real, productive work, helping your organization be successful!

Secondly, how would that poor woman feel if the boss met with his male subordinates behind closed doors, but his meetings with her were always with the door open? Not only would it inhibit the discussion of anything confidential (such as her performance appraisal), it would also invite any passerby to poke his head in the door and interrupt, implying the meeting with her wasn't particularly important.

Attorneys or human resource advisers may try to generally discourage one-on-one meetings because of the potential liability they perceive. They can afford to take a very conservative position because they are not responsible for the success of your company. They are only responsible for keeping you out of a lawsuit, so it's no skin off their nose that you can't carry on the ordinary course of business because of those restrictions. But that's why you can't run your business according to pundits, attorneys, or human resources. If you are responsible for the success of your department, team, division, or company, you must work successfully with women. And that means you have to be able to meet with them in private and one-on-one.

Here's another reason not to have different rules for different sexes: It's probably illegal. If someone tries to set company policy about meetings between men and women, it would be the height of sex discrimination to have rules that apply to one gender and not to the other. To allow meetings between males while denying access to females would be a violation of the employees' civil rights in private corporations as well as in government agencies.

FALSE CLAIMS

A less funny problem with the Graham/Pence Rule is that their concern is sinister; they assume that women are such devious people they will turn a friendly meal into an opportunity to inflict damage with a lie about what happened. Let's talk about that elephant in the room.

You may be genuinely worried that something bad can happen to you: a woman misinterprets something you say, she has designs on your job, she gets mad at you and decides to take revenge, she's delusional and makes a bunch of stuff up, she—ahhhh! Calm down. The likelihood of that happening is slim. Very few women make serious false claims of sexual misconduct, and nearly all are revealed as liars. Numbers vary, but they are low. You'll hear the odd "that's harassment!" accusation when someone doesn't understand what real harassment is, but I personally know of more cases of unreported harassment than the very small number of false claims I encountered. Fear mongering about false claims reflects a misogynist culture. People should be more worried about how badly female employees are treated by their repugnant male bosses and co-workers than about false accusations.

Most working women are reasonable, thoughtful people. They just want to have a job or a career and an okay time at work. You can't have a good relationship with them if you treat them with distrust. They also know that no one is perfect. If you make a mistake and say something you shouldn't have, they're not going to sue you. Especially if you apologize.

MITIGATING RISKS

That said, there are ways to protect yourself. The best way to avoid having troublemakers in your midst is not to hire them in the first place. I find companies don't devote enough energy to perfecting a hiring process that will result in great hires. Somehow we always seem to be too busy or too casual to really do it right. We'll talk more about hiring in the chapter on management.

Another great way to protect yourself is to read the rest of the book. It will not only educate you about what constitutes sexual harassment and its gray-area relatives, it will also expose you to how men and women can work well together, build trusting relationships, and develop partnerships that can last a lifetime.

CALLING ON YOUR BRAIN

Another (and worse) problem with advising men not to meet with women is because the obvious corollary is don't hire women. LeanIn.Org didn't ask whether men would hesitate to hire women now, but it didn't need to. Guys are too smart not to have thought of that. Look, there's another elephant in the room!

We've already debunked the "you should hire women because they're more caring" baloney. I call BS on the other reasons thrown in by various interested parties—that women are more collaborative, more creative, and more intuitive. Besides painting all women with the same brush, we've all seen counter examples. Those hyperventilating arguments don't really help us.

Vested parties like to claim that companies with more women in leadership positions experience greater profitability. Allegedly, you should put women on your board to give your shareholders a better return. Some studies show that companies with more women are more innovative. Others claim that women can temper risk-taking at a company (which somehow would have prevented the financial meltdown of 2008; apparently, if only we'd had less testosterone on Wall Street, we would have been fine).

The thing is . . . I'm not convinced. Why? Because you know how studies go—one year they say one thing; another year, they say something else. What if next year the composition of the companies included in the studies changes, and companies with lots of women perform poorly, then what are we going to say? If some rogue researcher comes back with contradictory conclusions, what are we going to do? Fire the women? It's dangerous to make arguments like that.

Here's what you can rely on—your brain. Let's just use it for a doggone second. Women make up half the population. You would be doing yourself and your company a big disservice if you simply

17

ignore all the talent in feminine packaging. Unless you think that every woman is inferior to any man, you'd better include them in your candidate pool. That's the real reason to hire women: There are great ones out there.

YOU

This is the scene where you fly in and save the day. If we put aside all the craziness, common sense tells us that to hire only from half the talent pool in the country would be dumb. The value that you get from hiring a skilled woman outweighs the potential down-sides, which are mostly made up by hysterics anyway. You don't want to miss out on the chance to build productive, collegial re-lationships with some incredibly talented women because of the vitriol of the past year.

This is worth figuring out. If working with women makes you uncomfortable and working with them one-on-one makes you even more uncomfortable, you're going to have to practice. Proceed with caution, listen, and don't try anything weird. Over time, you will become more accustomed to such private interactions. When you become more skilled at working with women, you open up a world of opportunity that many men will miss out on. I hope you take advantage of such potential. When I think back on my career, my greatest joy came from what we—men and women—were able to accomplish. We wouldn't have been as successful without each other.

First Impressions

A thousand words will not leave so deep an impression as one deed.
~ Henrik Ibsen

L et's dig into some specifics, shall we?

PLEASED TO MEET YOU

When you are introduced to a female colleague, vendor, customer, consultant, admin, anything, shake her hand. Other countries have different customs, but in the United States, we shake hands. Now I'm going to ask you to do something exceptional. Shake her hand as though she were a man. As long you're not one of those mouth breathers who think you need to crush a man's hand until his bones grind against each other, just shake her hand as though she were a guy—a nice firm, up-down-and-done.

Some time ago, I asked a recruiter what I should be training my clients on, and she said grumpily, "Teach them how to shake hands, for God's sake." She demonstrated what candidates do wrong by extending her hand and giving me the classic wet-noodle shake when you have to flap the other person's arm as though you were shaking out a rug. "Yech," she said.

Here are some more yechy things men do. Please put your hand all the way into a woman's hand; don't just grasp her fingers and shake those as though she were some fragile lady, incapable of a real handshake. Any action that calls out her gender is not helpful. You've just sent the message, "Oh, I see you are a woman so I can't shake your hand properly." That makes her feel bad. In a social situation, perhaps women are okay with being treated "like a lady," but at work, not so much.

Shake with your right hand, don't hold on too long, and don't cover her hand with your other hand as though she were grieving. That's strange. You don't know her that well yet. Also, please, don't do anything squirrelly with your finger in her palm. And please, please don't raise her hand so you can kiss it. If I had a quarter for every weird handshake I've gotten from a guy, I could buy lunch. Stand out by being matter of fact and not doing anything icky.

LOOK AT HER FACE

Don't check her out. There may be forces in your so-called brain that encourage you to inspect her, but don't. Women notice where men's eyes go, and they complain when men stare at their private parts. Ever seen those T-shirts that say, "MY FACE IS UP HERE" with an arrow pointing up to her face? It's tied in with women's complaints about being "objectified," which I notice men sometimes seem confused about. "After all," they say, "I'm just appreciating her body. Why should she be offended by that?"

Here's the problem, at least as I see it. When you check out a woman's body in a workplace setting, you have introduced an inappropriate sexual message. She's there to work, not to be considered as a potential sex partner. Even worse, since you have just met her, you are sending a message that her primary asset is her body—not her brain, not her experience, and not her education—which, frankly, is downright discouraging for a professional woman.

Suppose that someone asked you to take off your shirt in a job interview. Unless it's a modeling job, I bet you would find that alarming. You would wonder exactly what attributes the interviewer was looking for. This attitude that we have in America that a woman's primary value lies in her beauty and not in her brain has simply got to stop. So I'm counting on you to make that happen. I'll give you a couple years 'cause it's a tough problem.

ADDRESSING WOMEN

Be sensitive to calling women by their first names if men are being referred to by their titles. It's amazing how often (you'll notice it now that it's been pointed out to you) women in a group will be referred to as "Jan" or "Robin" while the men are called "President This" or "Dr. That" or "Judge Whatever."

INCLUDING WOMEN

Be careful about your assumptions concerning the relative rank of the people you are being introduced to. Stories abound about some poor doofus vendor or consultant who assumed one of the men in the room was the senior leader only to discover that the lone woman outranked them all. "Hahahaha," say the women when they tell this story, although they and we know it isn't that funny.

Women sometimes complain that, even when it is clear they are the decision makers, vendors or consultants will continue to talk exclusively to the guys. That is bad, and don't be that guy—but I'm a little sympathetic. Female executives can be intimidating, causing everyone to be afraid to talk to them. I encourage my female clients to relax and make everyone feel better, but I can only do so much. In any case, make sure that you're including the women in your remarks.

THE INVISIBLE WOMAN

Be especially gracious if a woman hasn't been introduced at all but is left to stand there as though she's not corporeal. You will win points by turning to her and saying, "I guess we haven't met. I'm The-Only-Guy-Here-With-Manners." No, I'm kidding. Don't say that, but do introduce yourself and make her feel part of the group. Maybe she'll leave her jackass colleagues and come work for you.

SAY HI AND INTRODUCE YOURSELF

I can hear you wondering if you can spontaneously introduce your-self to a woman you don't know in the lunchroom or the hallway. Yes! The good news is that because you are a professional, you are free to be friendly to a woman without the implication that you are trying to hit on her. It's actually quite liberating. I wouldn't wander around introducing yourself only to women—that would be pecu-liar—but it's really okay to approach a woman, just as you would a man that you don't know, and introduce yourself. We'll talk more later about not hitting on her.

Quick story: At my first job out of graduate school, I worked for a company that owned two buildings connected by an under-ground tunnel. When I walked through the tunnel, I noticed that the guys, especially the young guys, coming in the other direction wouldn't even look at me, not to mention say hello. I couldn't figure it out; I was coming from administration and they mostly worked in engineering, but was I so terrible looking that they couldn't even look at me? It made me feel uncomfortable and unwelcome. One time I walked through with another female colleague, and this time the guys practically plastered themselves along the wall to avoid getting close to us and studied the ceiling to avoid looking at us. No one said hello. My colleague explained it. "They never see women down here," she said. Ahhhh. I'll tell you what, I sure would have felt better if one of those guys had just said hello.

SMALL TALK

I notice a lot of guys do this when they talk to women at social or networking events: They engage in *really* small talk. If they're talking to another guy, they'll talk about work, news events, sports, or important personal affairs, like buying a house or college ex-penses. When a woman walks up to join the conversation, they turn into jokers, kidding her about some old history or querying her about her family or hobbies, all safe topics. This represents a real loss for the woman who needs to establish a professional rap-port with the guys and gather the same kind of information from an informal exchange as guys do. If you catch yourself moving to lighter topics as soon as a woman shows up, scold yourself for you. sexism and try to move the conversation back to more serious issues.

This is not always the guys' fault. I have certainly overheard women talking to each other about vacations they have just gone on while behind them a couple guys are hashing out a way to reprice options. Which is more valuable, leaving an event having learned about another company's repricing policy or with dreams of Patagonia?

I often lament how stupid our conversations are; it's such a waste. If you assume that your conversationalist can teach you something, you can have more interesting exchanges. Try to have a discussion in which you change your mind about something—that is proof positive that your exchange was meaningful.

COMMON COURTESY

It's funny to me how preoccupied some women are with who opens a door. They'll ask me if it's okay when men open doors for them or if maybe they should be insulted and refuse to walk through. Gee. I think most guys hold the door for a woman because they've been told that's what they're supposed to do and that it's polite. I tell the women to walk through and say thank you. If a woman holds the door for you, the same goes for you: Walk through and say thank you. Salaries, promotions, equal opportunities, sexual harassment, unethical behavior—those should be big deals to women (and men). Door opening isn't. Not everyone will share my view, but I don't think you should be paranoid about opening a door for a woman. If someone gets offended, she needs to grow up.

LASTING IMPRESSIONS

You've gotten a few tips here about introductions, shaking hands, where to look, and what to talk about. Those will serve to make a good first impression. In the next chapter, you'll hear more about talking and listening. That will help you to make a good lasting impression and further your efforts to build a robust professional relationship.

Listening and Talking

Standing up at a podium to denounce sexism is great,
but it's the day-to-day actions that yield the best results.
~ Elissa Sangster, Forté Foundation

Much of our interactions at work involve verbal communication. Given the subtlety of language, word choice, innuendo, tone of voice, eye contact, facial expressions, and possible misinterpretation of all the above, what could possibly go wrong?

LISTEN UP

The biggest complaint from my female clients is that they aren't listened to at work. They feel ignored, both in small ways when their comments in meetings come to naught, or in big ways when their recommendations fall on deaf ears. Some of that might be on the women. Sometimes they don't make their arguments well, aren't persistent enough, or don't speak up at all. However, women are routinely ignored in too many workplaces. Sadly, I think it's further evidence that a lot of men aren't interested in what women have to say, don't find them credible, and don't enjoy having to listen to them.

I would ask you to consider your own behavior and those of others when a woman is speaking. Do other men start talking among themselves when a woman speaks up? Do they all sud-

24

denly develop an insatiable need to check their phones? Do they interrupt her multiple times to regain control of the meeting? Do they wait for her to be finished and then pick up the discussion as though she has said nothing? If she has raised a concern, do they brush it aside and move on? Those behaviors don't go unnoticed, and they contribute to women deciding it's not worth it to talk in meetings at all.

If you suspect that your male co-workers don't listen to women as a matter of routine, watch yourself to see if you make that mistake. You may have to make a conscious effort to slow down when a woman is speaking and focus. Practice active listening by exercising nonverbal signs of participation, such as nodding or making eye contact. Reacting to her input is also a meaningful way to show that you are listening. If you oversee the meeting, when she finishes speaking you can thank her for her remarks or make an appreciative comment.

To me, a real reaction is superior to a cursory thanks, and she should prefer that too, although it may be hard for her to take. If you want to correct or clarify something she said, you should do so to move the discussion forward, but you should do it in a way that doesn't shut her down. Examples abound of women being dissed in meetings, and, once again, they often respond by falling silent. Instead, by actively including her in the discussion, you are demonstrating to the group that it is acceptable for her to talk.

If you're really brave, you can call guys on their rude behavior. After all, as one man said helplessly to me during a discussion about the treatment of women, "Some guys are just oblivious." If they try to run over her without acknowledgment, you can say, "Wait a minute. I think Cheryl has raised a valid point." Use her real name if it's not Cheryl ☺. After you've done this a few times, I hope they get the message that your meetings welcome all to participate and that everyone's input is appreciated. I expect great stuff will come out of those conference rooms.

YOU LISTEN UP

Sony recently announced a leadership training program for women to "amplify their voices." If that sounds like an okay idea, you haven't yet grasped how times have changed. The reaction was swift and critical. People said the announcement was tone-deaf and that the women's voices were *fine*, thank you very much. I'd advise caution about implying that only women need help getting heard in meetings; some men are pretty quiet too, and perhaps some men need to listen more.

"I JUST SAID THAT"

Here's a special problem I hear about all the time. A woman will tell me that she made a point in a meeting, and nobody paid any attention. A few minutes later, a guy made the same point, and then everyone congratulated him on his brilliant input. This is so common that the *New Yorker* published a cartoon in which the chairman of a meeting remarks, "That's an excellent suggestion, Miss Triggs. Perhaps one of the men here would like to make it." This phenomenon makes women mad as heck.

I give women a bunch of advice about this because it is such a common complaint. I train them to re-evaluate how they spoke because perhaps the meaning was vague or garbled. I teach them how to jump back into the conversation to drive the idea forward. And I counsel them to be generous and not worry about getting credit for every little idea. But now that I have your ear, I can ask you to help them out. Pay attention to what women say in meetings. Sometimes they have good ideas.

WOMEN TALKING TOO LITTLE

In my experience, it was more common for women to speak very little in meetings and only slightly more in one-on-one meetings. No surprise, since many men give off clues that they don't like listening to women. Plus a meeting can be a real pressure cooker when male participants strive to dominate the discussion. If you're looking for input from all your colleagues, however, you need to encourage women to speak up and state their minds. Some women know they are supposed to contribute, so they choose the safe route of only offering support for the prevailing view. That is also objectionable because it's just talk with no thought. It will be especially important to make room for your female colleague if she is raising a point that conflicts with the consensus thinking. That is a very dangerous position for her professionally, and she may need some encouragement to stand her ground.

Early in my career, I erred on the side of staying silent in meetings. I was young and hadn't grown the big mouth that I have today. It seemed more effective to provide input off-line and use others as my mouthpiece when I didn't have to compete with the guys for air time. Or so I told myself.

When I served on an all-male (except for me) committee, the senior executive who chaired the meetings came to see me one day. After some chitchat, he said, "I need to tell you something. I sit in meetings with you, and I look at you, and I wonder what you're thinking." Wasn't that a graceful way to tell me I had a bad, lazy habit? It was hard for me to become an active player in meetings. I was nervous and worried about saying the wrong thing, especially when I was offering an opposing view. But I had support and felt I had been told that it was part of my job, so I forced myself. You too can be that gracious supportive senior executive for women you work with.

CALL HER OUT

Later in my career I was disappointed when women wouldn't speak up in meetings. Sometimes they would ask to be invited to a meeting and would attend but then not say anything. When I became more senior, I used a tactic that might work for you. I would directly ask for their contribution in the meeting. I would say, "Christine? Did you have any thoughts about the discussion today?" Most of the time, they did have thoughts, and I was often surprised at how insightful they were. Imagine that, women in meetings listening and thinking often do have something valuable to add. If that tactic works for you, you may find you have better meetings. In addition, you have sent a great message to your female colleagues that you value their input. That single thing can make a big difference in how women perceive their work environment.

If you call on a woman who hasn't spoken up, do so in a way that signals that her input is valued. Be polite and consider her comments thoughtfully. It's common for women to speak too softly to be heard, and sometimes other meeting participants will lose interest if they can't hear her. Ask her to speak up. Smile at her. If you make it safe for her talk, she is more likely to take the initiative in the future and maybe even speak a little louder. Don't let people get in the habit of ignoring women in meetings. Diversity is most valuable when everyone speaks and everyone listens.

WOMEN TALKING TOO MUCH

I frequently hear men complain about how much women talk, especially outside of work. I find men often are quite resentful of a woman who does speak a lot and refer to her as "dominating" the conversation. In addition, they can be highly critical of her input, particularly if she talks about herself or her experience. Similarly, other women can resent a woman who talks a lot, especially if she expresses herself forcefully or confidently.

If you find yourself chafing against a woman's verbal behavior, ask yourself if you wouldn't mind the amount or style of talking if it came from a man. You may be suffering from sexist expectations of how you think a woman "should" behave. That's not to say that some women aren't obnoxious verbose know-it-alls, but you should be cautious about labeling her as one before you have considerable evidence to support your view. The next chapter contains more information about self-assessment for sexism.

THE SILENT TREATMENT

Sometimes men will ice women out of conversations to send the message that they are unwelcome. No surprise—that hurts. Several women explained to me that guys will come into the office in the morning and say hi to everyone except the women. One woman said her newly assigned boss studiously ignored her and went out of his way to never speak to her unless spoken to. Those actions— or nonactions—are mean and feel like a form of hazing. I wouldn't expect anyone who has picked up this book to be guilty of such cruelty, but it may be eye-opening to hear how some men treat women in the workplace.

MANSPLAINING

This term came into common usage a few years ago, but it's worth reviewing because I find men often don't understand why it's offensive. It refers to a situation in which a man, for no apparent reason, takes it upon himself to expound on a topic to a woman who, for all he knows, may know more than he does about it.

If, for example, a man explains to a woman how to correctly pronounce her name, that is mansplaining. One woman reported that guys coming to her booth to place bets (she worked at a racetrack for fourteen years) would routinely explain to her how betting worked. I was surprised when a male relative started explaining climate change to a woman who has a PhD in geology from Caltech. One guy explained to a postmenopausal woman the symptoms of menopause. A childless male relative began explaining to me how a mother feels about her children (I have two kids).

I wonder what these guys think they are doing—if their brains are working at all. Their opening position appears to be that they know more about something than any woman ever could. Even when the women are clearly in a position of authority on a topic, the men continue to open their mouths and expose their ignorance. Are they simply more comfortable talking? Is it a way to puff themselves up? If they think they are impressing the women they are lecturing, they are sadly mistaken. The usual reaction is a giant eye roll.

If an exchange of information ensues, I wouldn't consider that mansplaining. I would interpret some occurrences of so-called mansplaining as a guy stating what he knew about a topic to see if he was missing something without asking outright to be corrected or enlightened. If the woman stays silent and doesn't challenge him, he might be unfairly charged with mansplaining. But I have seen assertive guys begin a monologue about a topic without it ever crossing their mind that the woman in front of them is in a far better position to talk about it. Of course, you would never be so foolish.

)ON'T COUNT"

>mplaint that I hear from women with surprising frequen-
ɪat a guy will tell a woman that she can't speak for women
ᴠᴇᴄᴀᴜse, in his words, "You're not like most women." Apparently
he judges her to be atypical, so she isn't allowed to speak on the
experience of being a woman. That *is* pretty galling. Why would he
get to decide that?

PLAYING "DEVIL'S ADVOCATE"

The more experience I have, the more pointless that seems to me.
It can be a real time-waster. If someone has a concern, they should
say so. I see men use this ploy to get a rise out of woman or to
avoid challenging her directly when they disagree with something
she said. Check yourself if you find yourself resorting to this pas-
sive-aggressive tactic. And I'd try to get your colleagues to take
real positions instead of hiding behind this assumed role. Women
shouldn't object to being challenged, and it's better for the group if
people put their cards on the table.

BODY LANGUAGE

I'll throw this one in here because it shows up in meetings. Researcher Amy Cuddy encourages individuals to make themselves
"bigger" to feel more confident. She suggests you spread your legs
out, take up lots of room, and put your hands behind your head. I
think this is great advice *before* you give a presentation, go into a
meeting, or give an interview, but not such great behavior during
the meeting or interview. It's too obvious (some people call it
"manspreading"), and it rubs people the wrong way. One woman
said that The-Guy-Talking-In-Meeting-Spread-Out-All-Over-
The-End-Of-The-Table should be a meme it was so prevalent. Yet
one more thing for you to be aware of.

TOO LOUD

Finally, women complain that men are simply too noisy at work.
They laugh uproariously, shout across rooms, bang on things, im-

pose their music on people, and yell into their cell phones. Some of this feels a little unfair and smacks of women being generally irritated with men, but I thought I'd pass it along.

SOME BASICS

What we've covered in this chapter is fundamental and important. Listening to women, making space for them in a discussion, giving them credit for their ideas, and calling guys out on their bad behavior—those are giant steps in the right direction.

Check Yourself for Sexism

Both men and women should feel free to be sensitive. Both men and women should feel free to be strong . . . it is time that we all perceive gender on a spectrum not as two opposing sets of ideas.
~ Emma Watson

This chapter will give you some food for thought about how we expect men and women to behave. We'll also give you a test to see if there are times when you treat your co-workers differently because of their gender. I'll start by asking for sympathy for the challenges that professional women face in today's workplace.

GENDER BIAS ANYONE?

We have been socialized to expect certain behaviors from men and other behaviors from women. When employees act in ways that defy those expectations, we may find them unattractive or even unacceptable. To be successful, a professional woman must display behaviors that were traditionally more associated with men. She must express herself in clear, emphatic tones. She has to make hard decisions that may offend some male egos. For such gender-bending, she might be criticized, by both her male and female colleagues. I call this the Executive Woman's Dilemma—a female manager must demonstrate strong leadership characteristics, but those are often negatively perceived in a woman.

If you react badly to a woman's behavior, step back and ask yourself if it would be acceptable if she were a man. If yes, your reaction may reveal some subtle gender bias on your part. Others may fall into that trap as well. Gender bias is especially damaging during the hiring process, on performance evaluations, and while selecting vendors. Strong female performers rub some people the wrong way. Someone's outdated view of women shouldn't cause you to lose good candidates, employees, or contractors.

THREADING THE NEEDLE

Advice for executive women often sounds contradictory: State your position, but not too strongly . . . Be decisive, but be sure to include others . . . It's okay to be ambitious, but don't let it show . . . Do a bit of this, but not too much . . . Just be perfect, all right? Women complain to me about this double standard. "My manager told me I needed to speak up in meetings, but then he told me I'd better tone it down." "If a man had said what I said, he wouldn't have been criticized for it." "I asked for a raise, and they said I was being too aggressive." Other confused women say to me, "But I don't want to act like a man," and I say back, "And you shouldn't. That would be counterproductive."

If stereotypical male and female behaviors each form a circle, the overlapping area (or the intersection for those of you who remember your Venn diagrams) represents behaviors that are socially acceptable for both men and women. If you look at the overlapping area just right, it resembles the eye of a needle. In my observation, successful professional women are usually using behaviors that stay mostly within that eye; they are not overly feminine, nor do they demonstrate overtly masculine behaviors. It's not easy to thread the needle. Many women get so fed up with this catch-22 that they quit work altogether.

I bring this up to ask for a bit of empathy for the tough row that women must hoe at work. I can't ask you to completely adjust your expectations about male and female behaviors—that would require a brain transplant—but perhaps these revelations will make you more sympathetic to the dilemma often faced by your female colleagues.

NOT UNIQUE TO WOMEN

It's worth mentioning that men, especially foreign men, occasionally tell me that they find my advice for women helps them too. Obviously, not everyone is comfortable in an American-male culture. When we ourselves are at ease, it's easy to forget how lucky we are. We must keep an eye out for our colleagues who don't share our background, don't speak our language, or haven't had a similar cultural upbringing.

GENDER MATTERS

Two stories from colleagues about times they mistook someone's gender are revealing. In one case, a man thought a consultant he was working with remotely was a woman because his name was Sharon. When he realized that he was working with a man, he was very surprised. As he thought back over his interactions, he realized that if he had known earlier that the consultant was a guy, he would have invited him out for a beer when he was in town. It never occurred to him to do that with the "woman."

In another situation, a friend assumed that an acquaintance she had met by email was female because they were both members of a women's organization. She suggested that they get together the next time she was in Boston and then was appalled to discover that her new friend was a man. She was terribly embarrassed that her invitation might be misconstrued and couldn't figure out how to get out of the social obligation.

Here's a test for you: What should my colleagues have done? Did you say they should have gotten together for a social drink with their new colleague, male or female? Yes! A-plus for you. Already I can tell the world is getting better.

WHAT IF HE WERE A SHE?

Try this out: If you would do the following with a male co-worker, should you also do the same with a female colleague?

Meet one-on-one? Yes.
Go out for a drink to unwind? Yes.

34

Travel together to a company event? Yes.
Go to a baseball game? Yes.

Likewise, if it's something you wouldn't do to a guy at work, should you do it to your female colleague?

Give him a neck massage? No.
Talk about his hairstyle? No.
Ask him to get you a cappuccino? No.

This mind experiment can also point out some places where you might not be treating your male employees as professionally as you should. If it's something you surely wouldn't do with a woman at work, should you do it with a male colleague?

Insist that they go to a strip club? No.
Quiz them about their sex life? No.
Play drinking/betting games while golfing? No.

I'm sure your brain is working overtime to think of an exception to catch me out. Keep thinking. It's a pretty good rule. If we're looking for equality in the workplace, it does mean that we want to treat men and women the same. Swapping the gender tables can open your eyes to ways to improve the civility of your entire workplace.

HANGING OUT

Getting to know your colleagues in semi-social occasions makes for much stronger relationships and builds teamwork and trust. Be sure to invite women to the guys' events. It's not up to you to decide if it's appropriate for them; the women get to decide that. It would be nice if you chose events that weren't openly hostile to women like strip clubs or parties with escorts, but women may be more game for a golf outing or a speedway event than you think.

HOW TO BUILD GOOD RELATIONSHIPS

You should strive to build informal collegial relationships with your female co-workers just as you do with your male co-workers. If you do, you may be the first guy that they've had that kind of relationship with, so proceed thoughtfully. It takes time and effort, but it is usually possible and almost always worthwhile. I suggest spending time with them: drop by their offices, call them on the phone, and exchange information. You may have to make the first move, but, if you keep your interactions professional, your colleagues will not misinterpret your friendliness as a suggestion for a date.

As the women get to know you, your relationships can become more easygoing, natural, and genuine. You will all feel more comfortable providing useful feedback that will help everyone improve. Work becomes more rewarding, not to mention more fun. When women become part of the network, it positions them for information, potential assignments, and sponsorships. We hear men say that they don't promote women or put them on boards, simply because they don't know them as well as they do their male colleagues. Make sure that you know your female colleagues just as well as your male colleagues. That gives your company or associates access to untapped talent.

Relationships built on trust are sturdy and can endure a blow or two. Trust provides flexibility because the women will give you the benefit of the doubt if your behavior surprises them. That can be extraordinarily beneficial if you screw up and let your sexism show. If your relationships are solid, the women will laugh it off, and you can all get back to work.

WHAT IF THE WOMAN DOESN'T PLAY ALONG?

Here are typical criticisms I hear men make of their female colleagues: "She's too serious. She doesn't hang out with us. She's easily offended." And the kicker: "She lacks self-confidence." Gee, I can't imagine why! But those are important insights. Some women are so uncomfortable at work that they treat the men as the enemy and are unfriendly, even hostile. They are on the watch for slights or put-downs and react unpleasantly to jokes and banter. They hide behind formal emails and only interact with their colleagues in meetings. Heaven knows, they're never going to have a chuckle or go out for a pint.

At this point, can I ask for some understanding? Now that you know more of the challenges facing women in the workplace, can you see why they might act like that? We'll talk more later about poor behavior by women, but I hope that you would consider how you might break through such an edifice. Turning one of those unpleasant women into a productive team member who can relax and have more fun at work would be a significant success.

SOME EASY MISTAKES

A man sometimes attempts to turn a female colleague into someone he is more familiar with: his daughter, his mother, or his wife. Watch yourself for that. It's easy to slip into a way of behaving that you have experience with, but a professional relationship is different, and it will take practice to figure out what it looks like.

One senior woman pointed out that although many of her male co-workers were self-proclaimed feminists, they were quick to trot out their baggage when she challenged them. If she questioned them about their expense reports, they complained she was acting like their wife. If she reprimanded them, they said she was acting like their mother. I certainly saw my share of this common mistake. If she's acting in a professional capacity, don't take it personally. If you find yourself getting aggravated with someone because you think she's acting like your mother, that might be your problem, not hers.

Also, if you find yourself thinking mean thoughts about a woman you work with, you may have to analyze your internal demons to see if you're mad at her because of something a different woman did to you, either that morning or when she broke your heart in high school.

HIS AND HERS

I'm sure you wouldn't be so insensitive as to ask the female staff to make coffee or copies if that's not part of their job. Less glaring discrimination, but discrimination all the same, is sometimes observed when a woman is sent out of a meeting to fetch someone, implying that her participation is less valuable than the men's, or when she is asked to take notes or send emails. Sandwich jokes are inadvisable, too, no matter how funny your male staff would find them.

I noticed that junior employees were often given different assignments depending on their gender. Young male employees were given meatier projects that required travel, necessitated interactions with more senior leaders, or were broader in scope. Female employees were assigned tasks that were closer to home, more independent, or more structured. With your new perspective, you can now see how much more valuable the guys' assignments would be to their long-term career. Be conscious of such bias when you decide who will do what.

On a related note, I recently attended a Little League game and noticed that the coaches would provide only positive feedback to a female player. "Good stop," they said when she failed to make a play at first. "Good pitch," they said when she walked a batter. Their feedback to the boys was noticeably different. "Caden! You gotta make that play!" "Alec! GET UNDER THE BALL!" It occurred to me that I've observed the equivalent in the corporate world when guys were challenged with training and harsh feedback while women were ignored or received pats on the head and were otherwise not taken seriously. I'm going to just ask you: Who's going to get better?

IT COULD HAPPEN

Here's a side note: Even though she's a woman, she still might know about computers/coding/networks/your phone. It's a small point, but remind yourself not to assume that she's not a technical genius. She just might be.

WHAT ISN'T SEXISM

To flush out other ways men demonstrate sexism at work, I prowled around the internet for things that bug women. Some of it was stupid. One woman complained that men were the only ones who skateboarded through their office. Good grief, girlfriend, pick up a dang board and join the party.

One man complained that women insist on being treated like

one of the guys but then object when they are. I think he has a point. For example, a woman objected when a man said to her in a meeting, "Actually, that's not correct." I'm willing to take some guff about this, but I think you're allowed to say that in a meeting—and it's okay to say that to either a man or a woman. I am asking for special consideration for the women you work with, but that doesn't mean you have to treat them with kid gloves. They are still expected to be accurate and make arguments based on facts. Make sense?

BREAKING TRADITIONAL GENDER ROLES

We talked before about door opening and how it's not a big deal. Another question however is not so simple: Who picks up the bill? If it's a work event, the senior employee or the finance person should pay regardless of gender. If that makes you uncomfortable, too bad—you'll get used to it. Since the expense will be turned in for reimbursement, it's inappropriate for a male to pick up the tab for a more senior woman, no matter how gallant his intentions.

If it's a social occasion, you should trade off on who pays. You should not always pick up the bill when you go out with female colleagues; it implies that you're on a date. We'll talk more later about how you're definitely *not*. If the woman is consistently slow to reach for her wallet (and I have written very unhappily about how women are sometimes terrible at picking up the tab), I might try to jolly her into it by saying something like, "Everyone ready for another round? You going to get this one, Jennifer?"

She might be relieved if she didn't know how to gracefully intervene to pay. That happened to me once. I wanted to pay for a round in an English pub and was grateful when a colleague came with me to place the order (no way could I keep track of those bitters, ales, stouts, and lagers) but then let me pay. Easy-peasy.

CONSIDER THE PORN

Here's a touchy subject for you. Generally I'm opposed to telling people what they should watch on their phones. However, if you're in the habit of watching women being sexually subjugated and humiliated before you go to work every day, I wonder if it's hard not to impose those images on your co-workers once you get there. That's probably not conducive to an easygoing, respectful, dispassionate relationship that you're looking to establish with them. Habits are hard to break, but that one might be a good one to give up. I highly recommend the gym in the morning.

"GENDER-BLIND"

This chapter has encouraged you to treat men and women mostly the same. It also has provided a test to identify gender bias. Being gender-blind is impossible, but all of us can work on erasing negative sexism from our everyday behavior for the well-being of both men and women.

Words with Problems

"A woman needs a man like a fish needs a bicycle."
I really hate this expression. I bet fish would totally want bicycles.
~ Meg Cabot, *Princess on the Brink*

We apply certain words (well, insults mostly) almost exclusively to men and others almost exclusively to women. I'll bet you can think of several off the top of your head. Many words or phrases subtly expose our gender bias or disapproval. This chapter will open your ears and enhance your sensitivity to the power of words to imply, hurt, or confuse.

LOADED WORDS

We'll start with the A's. Over the decades, we have told, trained, and coached women to be "assertive." It was supposed to counter-act what we thought was women's tendency to be meek and not stand up for themselves. As usual, it turned out that women were smarter than we thought. Once they did try to assert themselves, they were reprimanded for being "aggressive." Countless women have shared with me how unfair it was that speaking up resulted in that accusation, particularly if they felt that men were not being similarly criticized when they behaved the same way.

In a study of 248 performance appraisals, linguist Kieran Snyder discovered that women received much more critical personal feedback than men did, 88 percent compared to 59 percent. Thirteen women were reprimanded for being "abrasive," a word that showed up in none of the men's reviews.

Moving on to the B's, I must bring up the b-word. Nah, I'm talking about a different b-word—"bossy." This word is typically applied to a school girl by peers who think she is ordering the other kids around. Sadly, women who are perceived to be overstepping their place in the workplace are also labeled with this unpleasant moniker. Even if the woman is in fact the boss and hence has the right to be bossy, people still don't like it.

And now for a c-word. I know what you're thinking. No, men sometimes tell women to "calm down," which often backfires. The reprimand implies that the woman is being emotional or irrational, which might really tick her off (just as it would you). Similarly, telling a woman that she is "overreacting," is probably inadvisable. That condescending attitude is why adults object to "whatever," the teenage anthem that simultaneously says your position is crap and refuses to engage. Some study said that 38 percent of Americans described it as the most annoying word in the English language. That's how effective it is.

A friend told me a related story. Although she had been promised that her computer would be set up by the time she started her new job, it wasn't ready on her first day. When she arrived on her second day, it still wasn't ready. She walked into her boss's office to see if he could remedy the situation. According to her, she said, "Mike, I still don't have my computer. Can you call someone to get it set up?" He picked up the phone, called the IT department, and said, "Jan is in my office—hysterical." I wasn't there, so I can't vow that she wasn't hysterical, but she is a fairly unflappable person. His use of that word really bothered her.

Another friend told me about a faculty member who argued in a public meeting that his department needed a new building because his was "menopausal." Bad. Word. Choice. Beware of using loaded words that imply gender stereotypes or sexist attitudes.

"ADORABLE"

Examples of gender-specific words abound once you start paying attention. A male newscaster called superstar snowboarder and Olympic and X Game gold medalist Chloe Kim "adorable." Another journalist scolded him for his word choice. "The point is that she can land back-to-back 1080's, not that she's adorable," she griped. I agree, but do you think it's possible to be both an awesome boarder and adorable? Of course, at work you would never call a woman "adorable," "sweetheart," "honey bun," "darling," or other endearments. The real question is how you get guys who do that to quit.

GUY STUFF

Some words seem to apply to guys exclusively. Terms such as "stand-up guy," "rock solid," the "right stuff," "A-player," even "good guy," seem difficult to modify to apply to women. Words, such as "organized" or "competent" or "capable" or "reliable," that I do hear applied to women—even in a positive way—suffer from a lack of pizzazz. Would you consider describing some of your female colleagues as "audacious" or "charismatic" or "enlightened" or "powerful"? Just asking for a friend.

"BOYS WILL BE BOYS"

We still hear this cliché offered as an excuse for sexist and stupid behavior toward women. The implication is that men can't control their immature impulses and, shucks, since we can't do anything about it, we shouldn't even try. And, besides which, aren't they cute? You should hate this demeaning expression and never let anyone get away with saying it.

DON'T CALL HER OUT ON HER GENDER

One common mistake I see is that men will call attention to a woman's gender. I recognize that men are often acutely aware of a female presence, but you're better off to set that aside. Don't ask for a woman's perspective or ask her to coach another woman or imply that she could do more with a male client than you could. Don't ask her to do anything you wouldn't ask a guy to do. You're pointing out that she's different—and maybe not in a good way.

Sometimes, the intention is innocent, but I would still ask, why even go there? A man approaches a group of women sitting together in the corporate lunchroom and calls out "Hello, beautiful ladies!" This isn't a crime, but why would you do it? The women might feel slightly flattered, but they are more likely to be uncomfortable or irritated that the guy is drawing attention to the fact they are all female. It's irrelevant. How much better it would be to say, "Hello everyone!" or to call them by their names. Remember that each time you make an issue of someone's gender, it drives a wedge between us.

WHAT DO YOU CALL 'EM?

As a society, we can't seem to figure out what to call female people. We swing from girls, gals, and chicks, to women, ladies, and a whole host of nasty terms. None seem quite right. They all seem loaded with innuendo in contrast to the simple word for a male human, "man," or its friendly cousin, "guy." Let's break it down.

"Lady" was historically a polite term for a woman, its male counterpart being "gentleman." "Lady" is often used to refer to a woman in her presence ("Give your ticket to the nice lady.") or to address a woman directly, although not always politely, such as "Hey, lady, watch where you're going!"

"Lady" can also be used to criticize someone for their behavior. It still amuses me to remember how an umpire reprimanded the pitcher on my softball team for "unladylike" behavior after she threw a bad pitch and uttered the f-word. It's easy to turn "young lady" into a reproach, such as "Listen here, young lady."

In my observation, "lady" can also have a pejorative tinge, such as "cleaning lady," where it is used to dress up a demeaning job. We have "lady of the night," "bag lady," or "cat lady" (quite different from "Cat Woman!"). And, let's not forget "my old lady." "Lady" can also point out the incongruity of a woman holding a certain position, for example "lady doctor" or "lady writer."

University of Cambridge professor Deborah Cameron argues that the distinction between "lady" and "woman" is that the former is associated with femininity or feminine activities, not with sexuality or even strength. She argues that "lady" is a euphemism, "a veil drawn over the grossness of female physicality, sexuality, and reproduction." For those reasons, and because we seem endlessly conflicted about women, "lady" lost favor with feminists, and "woman" gained in political correctness. As Cameron has pointed out however, "woman" carries a sexual connotation which some people consider impolite. Those speakers may hesitate to use the term in a professional setting, particularly in greeting. So, you are unlikely to hear someone say, "Well, hello, women!" I can imagine someone's discomfort in saying, "The women in the office are planning a surprise party," and expect they would try to rephrase it. Which brings us to the "girl" problem.

If "lady" has lost favor, "girl" has really lost it with the police of political correctness. Because it's also a term for a female child, using it to refer to a grown woman is considered insulting, in some circles. It's widely used by women to refer to themselves, as in "Girls' Night Out," or "It's just us girls tonight." Lately, "girl" has even been turned back into a feminist anthem with "girl power," "fight like a girl," and "you go, girl." We've had a veritable explosion of books and television shows with "girl" in the title. Women also frequently address each other as "girl," as in "Hey, girl, what's happening?" although I've heard myself say, "Hi, lady!" Some embrace the term "girls" as the female equivalent of "guys," which you'll hear as "guys and girls." In that context, you'll also hear "guys and gals." Which brings us to "gals."

Men sometimes reach for this term because they've been told "girls" is out, and they can't bring themselves to say "women" because it sounds inappropriate. Women also often use this casual term to refer to themselves. You'll hear women say, "Come sit with us gals," or "The gals are getting together after work." Substituting "women" in those phrases alters the tone, but "gals" presents its own problems. It's not used everywhere in the United States and has a southern feel which many might not be comfortable with. It's used more by older women, which implies that the "gals" are old girls, which some may find degrading in two ways: They're labeled as both old and as diminutive.

The what-do-we-call-them problem was amusingly brought again into the mainstream last year when singer-songwriter Keith Urban showcased a song he intended to be sympathetic to women. Sadly, he titled it, "Female," which caused comedian Stephen Colbert to issue his own anthem to women that he titled, "She-Person."

So, it's a mess. It's hard to find a word that doesn't trigger some sort of reaction. A friend says we should just call women "guys," and be done with it. It's common to hear a group of employees, including men and women, called "guys," as in, "Guys, let's all work together." But on this topic, there's always a counterargument, and some feel that the term leaves out the women in the room. With my linguist hat on, I can only observe what terms speakers use under what circumstances. But, in pursuit of my goal to improve relations between the sexes, especially at work, I hope there will come a time when we don't have to distinguish between men and women, and they will all simply become "people."

SPORTS IDIOMS

Colorful and evocative language is a delightful way to communicate, especially in business where our communication is often laden with senseless and boring jargon. Idioms can be lively, expressive, and a wonderful shorthand to communicate a concept in a subtle or humorous way. Take, for example, "three people can keep a secret, if two of them are dead," "that dog don't hunt," or "a fool's errand." Idioms and metaphors can be fun, but only when they are understood by everyone involved. Be aware that sports idioms, which I hear all the time in the business world, may be lost on people who are unfamiliar with sports.

To get the ball rolling, here's one whose meaning can be somewhat subtle: "not a team player." Under normal circumstances, this term means that a person doesn't work cooperatively with his or her co-workers, leading to a decrease in productivity. It could also be man code for "not one of us." Ellen Pao, then a junior partner at a venture capital firm in Silicon Valley, was said to not be a team player on a performance appraisal prior to her filing a sexual discrimination suit against her employer. It can also refer to an individual who isn't going along with the group's decisions, which might include unethical or inappropriate behavior. It's notable that many whistle-blowers are women, and I wonder how many of them were described as "not a team player" before the wheels came off. It behooves us to understand better what is going on when that description shows up on a performance appraisal.

A related term is to "play ball," as in "she won't play ball," meaning she won't go along with something. It's not always a criticism—but it probably is. When that accusation is levied at someone, it's worth thinking about why she might be resisting. Maybe she's being a jerk, but maybe there's a good reason that she is a holdout. Both expressions may be used against a woman who is being ostracized by the group.

STEPPING ALL OVER THE PLACE

I gave a talk awhile ago in which I made fun of business jargon and cautioned the audience about using sports idioms. A woman came up afterward and said that she had just been on a phone call with a human resources representative and an attorney in which they were critical of an employee for "not stepping up." I asked her if she thought the employee knew what that meant. "I hope so," she said, "because they're going to fire him for it!"

"Stepping up" is an ambiguous term because it has moved on from its original meaning to "step up to the plate." Not long ago, it simply meant to put yourself forward to lead an effort or take responsibility for something, like "Joe, I need you to step up to the plate for me. Can you take over the supervision of the night crew for this week while Jolene is out?" It didn't mean that you had to hit a home run; it was just doing something a bit extra.

The term has become more complicated and nuanced. Now I hear it used in much broader contexts where its meaning has evolved, especially for "*not* stepping up." Typically, I hear it used in a performance context where I worry that the object of the accusation isn't sure what he or she needs to change. A CEO is criticized for not stepping up when sales decline. *The Atlantic* wonders if Europe can step up. Silicon Valley is told it needs to step up.

The danger of this term is exemplified by the sad story of Recording Academy CEO Neil Portnow. During a panel discussion in 2017 about the lack of female representation in the music industry, Portnow said that women needed to "step up." Well, that's how the media reported it amid the ensuing uproar. Here's what he actually said: "I think it has to begin with women who have the creativity in their hearts and their souls—who want to be musicians, who want to be engineers, who want to be producers, who want to be part of the industry on an executive level—to step up, because I think they would be welcome."

All hell broke loose. He was blasted on Twitter that night, and the next day, a number of female executives signed a letter calling him out for his use of the term and calling for his resignation. Their letter said in part, "We step up every single day and have been doing so for a long time. The fact that you don't realize this means it's time for you to step down. Today we are stepping up and stepping in to demand your resignation." That's a lot of stepping around. Portnow issued a statement to clarify what he had meant, and the next day he announced a task force to examine bias in the Grammy process, but the damage was done.

I feel a bit sorry for the guy. He was speaking off the cuff, and I wonder if what he really meant was that women should "step forward," given his follow-up that "they would be welcome." In any case, it seemed like a great big hullabaloo out of proportion with his so-called crime. After all, Sheryl Sandberg, COO of Facebook and founder of LeanIn.Org, wrote a book about how women should "step up." Of course she called it *Lean In*. But still.

A side branch of "step up" are the terms "man up" and "woman up." These are used to tell someone to be braver and not act like a child. Because they are vague and emphasize the gender issue, I'd skip them.

WORDS THAT SOUND DIRTY

Some words should be okay but can be misinterpreted. Remember how in high school, when someone called somebody an "ass," people would act like that was a cuss word? You could argue till you were blue in the face that it was a perfectly acceptable word, but no go. And what about the word "niggardly"? Who wouldn't object to that?

Other phrases you might want to avoid for the same reason. "Open the kimono" is a phrase business development professionals use to mean sharing proprietary or confidential information with a potential partner. One school of thought is that the phrase originated with the samurai who would open his gown to show that he wasn't hiding any weapons. Others believe it refers to geishas. More, however incorrectly, believe it is both racist AND sexist. I'd avoid it.

A neighbor woman posted an ad for a "bed-cum-sofa" which drew several shocked responses from men. Yup, you'll have to find an alternative for that fine word.

There are those among us who find humor in any references to mastication, dongles, titular, uvula, or holes of any kind. Know your audience if you're trying to discuss something serious.

F*@% THIS F^CK!*G $H*T!

Sensibilities are changing, but many people still object to excessively profane language at work. Some women are offended and find it unprofessional, but so do lots of men. I'd try to rein in your blue language and encourage your staff to also. Keeping your cool is, well, cool.

STUPID BUSINESS JARGON

Novelist Martin Amis declared, "All writing is a campaign against cliche. Not just cliches of the pen but cliches of the mind and cliches of the heart." So it should be with you when you speak. If you express yourself clearly and simply, your message is more effective. Jargon drowns your message in burdensome wrapping that speakers mistakenly think sounds intelligent. Business jargon is the worst. Sometimes people talk in meetings and sound like blithering idiots. Distinguish yourself by your clear, concise speech that says exactly what you mean.

COMMUNICATION IS COMPLICATED

Words are subtle and can carry a boatload of hidden meaning. Tuning up your verbal skills can open your ears to the ways words are used to minimize, alienate, or ostracize women. Eliminating gender-laden phrases can turn you into a master of sensitivity in your interactions with your female co-workers. When you wield language with expertise, elegance, and precision, you open a path to better understanding between the sexes.

The Back Seat

Here we are, trapped in the amber of the moment. There is no why.
~ Kurt Vonnegut

We are in a climate now when everything you say can and will be used against you. A couple years ago, someone posted on the internet, "In 1816, women had no rights. In 1916, women fought for some rights. In 2016, women are always right." Some well-intentioned men have attempted to weigh in on the topic of sexual misconduct and have been punished for their good deeds. Sometimes you should err on the side of saying nothing about women in general, at least at work. I'm not talking about how things should be but how things are. Recent events have taught us that men can be unfairly castigated for opening their mouths.

I differentiate here between talking in general about women and gender issues and speaking up about a specific situation when you observe bias in the workplace. Pointing out ways to improve your workplace is an important intervention and should always be applauded when you feel inclined to help the cause.

THE MATT DAMON LESSON

After the truly disgusting information about Harvey Weinstein came out, actor Matt Damon gave a long slightly incoherent interview in which he attempted to address the complicated topic of sexual misconduct. He acknowledged the serious trauma the abused women had faced and said that weeding out "rotten apples" was progress. He said only a small percentage of the men working in Hollywood are abusive. He said there is a spectrum of bad behavior from patting someone on the butt to rape or child molestation. He said we are in the "bar fight stage" right now where it's all about retribution and wanting to punch people in the face, but that "when we go back to talking about our own growth and development as human beings, we have to get to a place where we deal with this with some reflection and dialog and reconciliation. Let's all grow together . . . Then I think we're making real progress." Pretty offensive stuff, right? Just makes you want to grind your teeth, doesn't it? I'm being facetious. I didn't think it was that bad. It turned out others disagreed. A lot.

That took place in December 2017. He was immediately attacked on Twitter and was told that a man simply can't understand the sexual abuse women face. One of his former female co-stars wrote, "It's galling when a powerful man steps up and stars [*sic*] dictating the terms whether he intends it or not" and "The time right now is for men just to listen and not have an opinion about it for once." One month later, after more bad press, Damon apologized for his remarks and said he was going to "get in the back seat and close my mouth for a while."

THE PUNCH IN THE FACE

Sometimes you should get in the back seat too, at least at work. If you find yourself saying anything that starts with "Women are . . ." or "Women should . . ." or "The problem with women is . . ." or really "women" anything, just shut your mouth right there and go back to work. You risk bringing nothing but ire upon yourself. In a similar vein, I would advise you to keep to yourself your opinions about working women or other female issues. Expressing your personal views about whether a woman should work outside the home or can have it all or whether there is a pay gap or gender discrimination is all just asking for trouble. I'd save it for an off-work conversation. Right now, you just can't win. Or even get a fair listen.

IT'S COMPLICATED

Even women can't get it right. After the highly successful #MeToo campaign, Catherine Deneuve and other powerful French women issued an editorial in which they criticized its fallout. They, too, were attempting to bring nuance to the discussion. They argued that public accusations have conflated sexual abuse with awkward flirting and that "this expedited justice already has its victims, men who were prevented from practicing their profession as punishment or forced to resign." They objected to the mentality that women need to be protected and worried that it would result in the loss of their sexual freedom. "Accidents that affect a woman's body," they wrote, "must not make her a perpetual victim." Amongst all of us, we probably have much that we would agree about, but in this atmosphere of zero nuance, only disagreement reigns.

ACCOUNTABILITY

Amid all the things Damon said, he tried to point out that when no amount of personal accountability is acceptable, the only recourse for a guy who is accused of misbehavior is to deny. When everything is painted with the same black brush, there's no room for apologies, explanations, or mitigating considerations. That's an interesting point. Of course, it was lost in the frenzy, but something for us to consider in these pages. We'll talk more about due process in the next chapter.

A LOT TO LEARN

Earlier in 2017, actor David Schwimmer and writer and director Sigal Avin made a series of six short films about sexual harassment and promoted them under the hashtag #ThatsHarassment. They are very well done, chilling, and revealing how wily guys can disguise harassment and manipulate women into tolerating and even becoming complicit in their behavior.

Schwimmer said that men have not been outspoken enough because of "an atmosphere of condemnation for any missteps" in talking about sexual misconduct. "Look, men have a lot to learn, but you're not going to learn anything without dialogue," he said. "Men commit the vast majority of rapes, sexual assault, and sexual harassment, so men have a special responsibility to do something about it and get involved." Amen to that.

JUST THINK ABOUT IT

If you harbor any question about how complicated and painful these personal interactions can be, even between mature adults, I dare you to listen to the seven-minute-long public apology that comic writer Dan Harmon offered his former employee for harassing her years earlier. He made this apology on his podcast *Harmontown* after she called him out on Twitter. After accepting responsibility for "damaging her internal compass," he said he had done things he wouldn't have if he had any respect for women. He begged his listeners to think about how easy it is to abuse power. His voice shook as he said, "Just think about it. No matter who you are at work, no matter where you work, in what field you're in, no matter what position you have over, under, or side by side with somebody, just think about it. Because if you don't think about it, you're going to get away with not thinking about it and you can cause a lot of damage." In a rare and heartwarming moment of compassion, she publicly forgave him and Twitter burst into applause.

THE FRONT SEAT

My caution about holding your tongue applies to speaking in general terms about women or about gender-related issues. In this red-hot climate, generalizations can kill you. However, I do hope that you'll speak up to talk about specific situations at your workplace. The stories about Matt Damon, David Schwimmer, and Dan Harmon show that men can make wise and insightful observations about the topic of sexual harassment. We need to hear from them about how to make our work environments better, and we should welcome them in the front seat. A man's voice can be a powerful force for reason and fairness.

What Is Harassment Anyway?

At its core, sexual harassment is unethical.
~ Wade Lindenberger

Sexual harassment has a legal definition, and it's worth reviewing as a starting point. It is defined as any sexually oriented behavior, demand, comment, or physical contact initiated by an individual at the workplace that is based on sex, and that is either (1) a basis for employment decisions (so-called "quid pro quo" harassment), or (2) sufficiently severe or pervasive so as to alter the conditions of employment and creates a hostile or offensive working environment. For example, with respect to quid pro quo harassment, an employer can't require a woman, either implicitly or explicitly, to have sex with him to keep her job, and a single instance can constitute sexual harassment. That part's pretty clear, right? It's the second type of harassment—hostile work environment—where things go gray.

The media make it sound as though all a woman has to do is cry harassment and a guy loses his job, but that's not true in the business world. To prove a hostile or offensive working environment is a high bar. It usually requires repetitive or regular bad behavior and the accusation of more than one woman. The corporate guys who have been taken down in the past year were repeat offenders, and many women came forward to back up each other's stories.

Most sexual harassment lawsuits are dismissed in court because the incidents are considered too minor or too few. The Supreme Court ruled that the behavior must be severe or pervasive. Posting a single sexually oriented calendar or a single pat on the butt or a single misogynistic joke does not constitute sexual harassment in the eyes of the law. That's not to say that they are good ideas or that they may not be against company policy. For our purposes here, it's good to know what's illegal, but more importantly you want to know what is advisable—and none of those are.

SEXUAL HARASSMENT TRAINING

In my experience, harassment training elicited more snickers than it resolved, and I hated those meetings because people would say such dumb things. Some of the most eye-roll-producing comments I've heard about men and women were uttered during sexual harassment training. It was depressing. Currently, most training is done online, adding to the perfunctory nature of the exercise and allowing employees to zone out during the lifeless videos. One would think anything about sex could be made interesting, but the trainers have found a way to bore us all.

The companies that hire the training companies are also complicit because of their CYA attitude and focus on the risk of liability, instead of promoting ways for people to work productively together and understand each other. Also problematic is that companies are disincentivized to get an objective evaluation of their training program because a poor report could be used against them. Also, companies often excuse their more senior leaders from the training, sending a blatant message to the underlings about how unimportant the training is. Men at the highest level of the company can be the biggest offenders. As a trainer, I find the whole ordeal completely annoying.

A colleague recently explained that everybody in her company turned off the audio on the online training program which then allowed them to advance through the slides more quickly to get to the "exam" at the end. And this was in a company where hidden cameras had been discovered under the desks of two female employees.

After three decades of mandatory training, it's also clear it hasn't worked. Complaints are higher than they have ever been. In 2016, the Equal Employment Opportunity Commission published a report on harassment in which they concluded that training has been a failure. Too many companies were only going through the motions of providing training so they could say that they did. One important recommendation the commission made was that training should include clear procedures about how to report sexual harassment, which is indeed a frequent omission. They also emphasized that the complaint process must be trusted. That's harder.

HUMAN RESOURCES

When women do drum up the courage to tell on their harassers, they are often ignored or the matter is swept under the rug by their managers or the human resources department. Company employees suffer from an inherent conflict of interest because a real investigation may open the company up to a lawsuit. In addition, companies are loath to go after an offender if he is a senior leader, well-liked, or otherwise a good performer. Reports of sexual harassment are hard to keep confidential, and word often leaks that there has been a complaint. People jump to their own conclusions about the veracity of the accusation, sides are taken, and the whole thing becomes a mess. No wonder the women won't come forward.

While I was working on this chapter, I was standing in an office hallway and overheard a woman on her phone. She said, "I don't want to go to HR because *I'm not like that*" (emphasis mine). For many reasonable women, that's the hurdle they must overcome if they decide to pursue a complaint because they know it will be negatively viewed. She spoke volumes in her short sentence.

Lastly, I found that human resource professionals were often not skilled in dealing with such sensitive issues, particularly if they involved someone higher up on the corporate ladder or turned into a he-said, she-said thing. Inappropriate comments were made, investigations were botched, the company went into lock-down mode, and details leaked. Those processes can all be made better, but it's going to take something more serious and sophisticated than just checking a box to say that all employees went through some negligible "training."

WHAT DO *YOU* DO?

What should you do if someone brings a complaint to you? I'm assuming here that you are not part of human resources; your actions will be different if you are. If you've gotten training about how to respond to a complaint, great. Most managers haven't, so this will get you started.

First, take her seriously. Sometimes a person just needs to be listened to. She will have to think carefully before she decides to formally report harassment, and she may need a sympathetic ear first. Assume for the moment that her claims are valid. You can say things like, "I haven't heard the other side of the story, but . . ." or "This is something we would have to look into . . ." or "If what you're saying is true . . ." This will make her understand that simply making an accusation won't result in action, but you are still communicating your sympathy.

Overly cautious attorneys will tell you not to apologize or acknowledge that she has been mistreated. I tell them to go jump in the lake. Give her a tissue if she's upset, and commiserate with her by saying, "I'm sorry this happened to you" or "I feel terrible about this" or "Thank you for telling me." Acknowledging her feelings may go a long way in defusing a significant conflict. She needs to understand that if there has been wrongdoing, the company is on her side. I believe that many sexual harassment suits would not have moved forward if the company hadn't acted like a total rat in the face of complainants' tears and misery.

"DON'T TELL ANYONE"

The employee may try to require your silence by only agreeing to talk "if you don't tell anyone." Make it clear that you will keep what she says confidential *but only if you **can***. There are some situations that you are required by law or company policy to report. She may decide not to tell you, but in my experience, she is always inclined to tell you anyway, which is a good thing. You do want to know what's going on in your company.

After she has told you, don't make light of what has happened to her. Don't defend the culprit by saying, "Oh, you know how Dave is" or "That's no big deal." It's a big deal to her. Don't attempt to dissuade her by saying, "Oh, you don't want to pursue this" or "This could come back and bite you" or "This is going to make my life difficult." It's unbelievable what insensitive things employers say to women who stand up to complain.

A PROCESS

She must understand that the company is obliged go through a specific process when there is a complaint. The company will decide if they must launch an investigation, the accused must have a chance to defend himself, and the complaint cannot be made anonymously. Your poor employee won't be happy to hear those things because they will make it harder for her. However, you must explain that simply accusing someone is not enough for the company to act. They must go through a formal process to be sure that justice is done.

In my experience, a complaining employee often hoped that someone else would just speak to the offender, and she would be left out of it. It won't and can't work that way. She will have to trust that her accusations will be taken seriously and that the company won't retaliate. In moving her toward an understanding of that, you can say things like, "The company takes this kind of thing very seriously" or "We have an established process that we follow to make sure we understand what really happened" or "You will have to answer questions and report this as part of our process." Those will help her understand the gravity of her situation.

In your shoes, I would encourage her to take a night to think about whether or not she wants to make a formal complaint. It won't be easy, and that should be made clear to her. But at this point, your role is to support her—and to let her know you do—in whatever decision she decides to make. Tomorrow is another day.

WHAT'S ISN'T SEXUAL HARASSMENT

One single sexual proposition doesn't constitute sexual harassment although many think it does. I don't approve of asking co-workers out or making a pass at them at work (more about that later), but it happens a lot. Just because it may freak women out doesn't mean it's illegal. What's more, I've heard a number of women say that once they said no, there was no retaliation. The guys didn't take it personally; they were just checking to see if there was interest. That's not a crime. You may find yourself in a situation when you have to explain that to a subordinate, in which case you'll want to do so in as sensitive and as kind a way as you can.

Some actions may not rise to the legal definition of harassment, but they could still be contrary to company policy if the company has specific written instructions about appropriate behavior at work. It behooves you to be familiar with those instructions if you're a manager, as you may be called on the spot to consider the magnitude of what someone has brought to you. May the force be with you. These situations are complicated, delicate, and horribly distracting. That's what you get for working with people and caring about them.

VICTIMS

I want to take a moment and acknowledge the millions of women who have been hurt and damaged by their bad experiences at the hands of men in the workplace. The #MeToo movement and its sister movement Time's Up have opened our eyes to the magnitude of sexual harassment in our country. Many women never tell anyone or formally report what happened to them out of embarrassment, because of fear of retaliation, because they hope it will go away, or for all the other reasons that people allow themselves to be victimized. I feel terrible for them and hope that this book can help in stopping that cruelty.

Why Didn't She . . .

*Time passed, and I learned in a hundred hard ways
how careful you have to be if you're born female,
how many places hold dangers—even just an ordinary office
with a respected male boss.*
~ Caitlin Flanagan

When you hear stories about women who were sexually exploited, it's too easy to think of what she *should* have done. It's hard to understand all the factors that complicated her situation in that moment. I hope this chapter makes us more sympathetic to women who get manipulated at work. We need our collective creativity and wisdom to provide them with real tools to defend themselves.

GOOD QUESTIONS AND GOOD ANSWERS

While I was working on my first book, I heard a story that amazed me. A young woman complained that when she slow danced with her boss, he put his hands all over her. I was astonished that she didn't object. And *why on earth was she dancing with him?* "Say NO," I ordered her in my book. "Stand up for yourself! Don't just suffer." Six years later, I know it's a lot more complicated.

After hearing enough unhappy stories, a reasonable person might find himself or herself saying, "Why didn't she just . . . say no? slap his hand away? tell him she didn't like it when he did that?" Good questions. Here are some reasons she didn't.

IT'S HER BOSS

This guy holds great power over her in the workplace. We're asking her to be beyond brave and trusting when we suggest that she either reject the offer to dance or object when he puts his hands on her. She certainly could be worried that he would be mad at her or feel rejected; neither is a sentiment that you want someone in charge of your salary, perks, promotion, or employment to feel toward you.

IT'S HER PAYCHECK

The threat of losing her job can be a powerful deterrent to speaking up. She may be a single mother or the main wage earner; she or her husband or her children may have health problems and medical bills. If she is otherwise happily employed, she may put up with bad behavior for the sake of paying the rent. She also may have experienced so much harassment in her life that she thinks it will be just as bad or worse someplace else.

SHE ALREADY SAID YES

An insightful friend also pointed out that once the woman had agreed to the dance, she may not have felt as though she could object to his hands because she was already in a compromised position and she was already complicit in the situation. I hate this argument, but I suspect that bad guys do this to move the goal posts and as leverage to get a little more of what they want. And some toxic cocktail of fear, shame, and guilt keeps the woman from objecting. We can see what a slippery slope this is.

SHE DOESN'T WANT TO HURT HIS FEELINGS

If her boss has treated her well in other ways (remembering that harassers can be charming and well-liked), she may not want to reject him. It's awkward to rebuff someone. Lots of women don't want to be responsible for making another human feel bad.

TRADITION

Raising objections and making waves are not considered positive feminine traits. We count on women to be peacemakers, to make others feel comfortable, and to smooth things over so their men don't end up in fistfights. We are surprised when women don't conform to these traditional expectations, and our surprise can turn to disapproval and even anger. Upstart women are advised "to fit in," "to try honey instead of vinegar," or "that you'd be prettier if you smiled." They know that telling someone an emphatic **NO** won't gain them any fans.

GOOD GIRLS

A lot of women at work are trying to get an A, as though they were still in school. They are trying to be good girls without understanding that what is appreciated in the workplace is different. A students don't tell off their teachers; they do as they're told; they follow the rules. Do you have any colleagues like this? It's very difficult for women with this mind set to refuse to do something that someone with authority wants them to do.

YOU WOULDN'T WANT TO EMBARRASS ANYBODY

The novelist Sue Grafton wrote, "I've taken enough self-defense classes to know that women, by nature, have trouble assessing personal peril. If followed on a darkened street, many of us don't know when to take evasive action. We keep waiting for a sign that our instincts are correct. We're reluctant to make a fuss, just in case we're mistaken about the trouble we're in. We're more concerned about the possibility of embarrassing the guy behind us, preferring to do nothing until we're sure he really means to attack."

Bingo. I have made this mistake myself with terrible consequences. Grafton's observation is so spot on, that I'll forgive her the "by nature" crack. If this behavior sounds incredibly stupid to you, be thankful that you're not this conflicted. Trust me, the desire for everything to just be okay is very strong.

BADASS WANNABE

It's easier to give advice when you're not in the moment. A female entrepreneur described a pitch session where an investor cornered her in a booth and pressed up against her before she was finally able to extricate herself and flee. Later, she remarked that if she had been asked prior to the incident how she would behave in such a situation, she was sure she would have bragged about how badass she would be. She said, "Then it just happened, and I did nothing."

POWER

I try to put myself in the shoes of these victimized women, and it's an easy fit. I too have occasionally gone along with bad behavior because I didn't want someone to get mad at me or make fun of me or hit me—not often, but I know the feeling. When disappointed or shut down, some men can be very vicious, taunting a woman for being a "spoilsport" or a "bitch."

A threatening undercurrent can also accompany interactions between men and women if the woman is aware of how much stronger the guy is. With the hint of potential violence in the air, she knows it would not go well for her. Some men use this to their advantage to intimidate by emphasizing their size or moving into a woman's personal space or standing too close or leaning over her. Bad guys ooze power and are very frightening because of their willingness to be cruel or violent, or both.

RETALIATION

Women may fear a retaliatory strike, or they've spoke up previously and know from experience how vengeful someone can be. Here's a story from the internet: "A guy I work with that's close to my dad's age constantly talks about how I look like his wife did when she was younger, but that she's not pretty like me anymore. I find it super odd. Also, I'm a super un-touchy person with people I work with, especially the men. The same guy forced me into a hug (he's at least twice my size) and wouldn't let me go because '(insert other female coworker's name here) lets me hug her so why don't you?' And then later called me a bitch because I told him to let me go." That story says it all. The woman was brave enough to tell a guy to let go of her. He denied her right to her own body and then called her a bitch. Is she more likely to simply put up with it next time some guy at work tries to hug her?

Retaliation is a big deal. Nearly 50 percent of the complaints to the Equal Employment Opportunity Commission are for retaliation. Employers don't like it when someone speaks up, steps out of line, blows a whistle, or makes waves—and, guess what, they retaliate. Lots of employees know this and keep their heads down, whether it's the assistant who puts up with some groping or an engineer who buries a test result or the CFO who looks the other way when the CEO misuses his company credit card.

NOT UNIQUE TO WOMEN

Lots of guys suffer from the same inhibitions and don't defend themselves, object, or speak up when they should. They too fear disapproval, name-calling, potential violence, or retaliation—all real scary reasons to toe the line. If we are successful in creating a civilized environment in which women flourish, maybe we will also protect others who are victimized but are suffering in silence.

WHAT ARE WE TO DO?

If we know that a lot of women are reticent to speak their minds, particularly when it comes to saying no, how do we proceed? It's no surprise that men are asking how they are supposed to behave toward women at work when they won't communicate clearly. It's frustrating. At this point in the book, you have already learned a lot of tools that can help you understand your female colleagues. Here are a few suggestions for occasions when you suspect women are holding back: You must listen harder. You will have to pay more attention. You may have to pick up on subtle non-verbal clues. You may have to ask about a specific situation in several ways and make sure you keep getting the same answer.

Let's look at two exchanges that end with very different results.

Clueless Manager Dude: *I have a project for you in London.*
Female Subordinate: *That sounds exciting.*
Clueless Manager Dude: *Great. We'll book you a flight for next week.*
[Subordinate goes home in tears.]

And

Smart Manager Guy: *I have a project for you in London.*
Female Subordinate: *That sounds exciting.*
Smart Manager Guy: *It means that you would have to work in London for six weeks. Can you handle that?*
Female Subordinate: *It would be a great opportunity for me.*
Smart Manager Guy: *True, but can you be away from home for six weeks?*
Female Subordinate: *You know, actually . . .*
Smart Manager Guy: *Yes?*
Female Subordinate: *I can't really be away right now. My dad is in the hospital, and I'm the only one to take care of him. I really wish I could do this project though.*
Smart Manager Guy: *I understand. Thanks for telling me. There will be other projects.*
[Subordinate goes home disappointed but relieved.]

COACHING

Knowing what you know now, you can also help your colleagues when you have the opportunity by coaching them to adopt a more direct communication style. In the workplace, we need efficient communication amongst colleagues to get our work done. We can be sympathetic to someone who has trouble expressing herself, but it would be better for everyone if she were simply more direct. If you successfully teach someone how to move out of her comfort zone, be brave, and convey her wishes and needs, you have done her a great service.

JUST ASK

Here's a novel idea. How about asking someone if it's okay if you do something? A colleague reported that a male co-worker said to her, "That's great news! Is it okay if I give you a hug?" She appreciated that he asked first. It might be awkward at times, but it's a tool to keep in mind.

If you're a manager, you may have to ask directly if someone is happy in their job. That is a fine idea with all your subordinates, regardless of their gender. If you open that door, however, you must be willing to listen to the answers. They may not make your day. Being a good manager is a hard job. It means facing problems that bad managers would ignore and hope will go away. The payoff is that if you are a good manager, your employees will appreciate you forever.

LESS CONDEMNATION

If we catch ourselves getting aggravated with women for not defending themselves or not making themselves clear, it's time to review this chapter. When people have power over us, they can deploy it in ways that are subtle and very dangerous. We shouldn't rush to judge a woman who doesn't appear to be acting in her self-interest.

As you build good relationships with your female colleagues, you can get to more direct and better communication, but that takes time. For now, you must listen for what is unsaid and make sure you have clear answers before proceeding.

We've now arrived at the eye-opening realization that your employees may be putting up with things that you do that they don't like, but they're not saying anything because they are afraid. Their decision to not object doesn't mean that they approve. That perspective will give you insight into what is really happening with the women (and men) you work with.

Rule #1

While forbidden fruit is said to taste sweeter, it usually spoils faster.
~ Abigail Van Buren

Following up on the idea that women often aren't in a position to defend themselves in the workplace, I'm going to hit you here with something that you just might hate. I deliberately didn't put this fundamental rule up front because I've gathered it might not be popular, and I didn't want to lose you early.

RULE #1: FEMALE COLLEAGUES DO NOT REPRESENT A ROMANTIC PROSPECT—EVER

No way, no how. Colleagues are off limits. I am inflexible on this because I have seen how much damage sex between employees can wreak on the parties involved, their co-workers, and the company. Adopting Rule #1 solves a lot of problems right off the bat. No flirting, no innuendo, no dating, no hookups. All interactions, either at the workplace or off-site, work related or social, are platonic and professional.

I get that this advice might disappoint your buddies and other, ahem, urges. Too bad. Different rules apply to how you behave at the workplace than to how you behave with women outside of work. Get your kicks someplace else. It will save you a lot of pain and agony in the long run. You're welcome.

BUT WHY WHY WHY?

If you'll hear me out, I'll explain why I have adopted this firm position over the years. In the beginning of my career, I didn't have such a strong opinion, but I have seen example after damning example of why sex in the workplace is a bad idea. Here are some reasons.

- ***They are distracting.***
Other employees get caught up in the tedious minutia of the relationship or wish it would all go away. The gossip, the fuss, and the spats are a drag when you're trying to get something done. God help you if one or both of the parties involved are married.

- ***They smack of favoritism.***
Employees may feel a romantic partner has an advantage over other employees (and they're probably right). They hate it when the company is no longer a meritocracy and that politics, especially sexual politics, have capsized what they thought was a level playing field.

- ***They damage your company's reputation.***
When people from the outside get wind of an internal affair, they may lose respect for the company or lose confidence in its management.

- ***They wreck your organizational chart.***
Romances create alliances that break down the careful separation of duties built into a good organizational chart. If the head of quality assurance is sleeping with one of the manufacturing engineers, your quality program has been compromised, and that should worry you.

- ***They increase turnover.***
One party might leave to escape the reminder of a soured relationship or because they have been wounded professionally. Even if the relationship survives, one party might leave to regain some privacy or because their internal opportunities are now more limited. Couples also want to

dissipate risk, and in case the company falters, they don't want all their eggs in one basket.

- *They invite retaliation.*

When either in the relationship gets fiddle-footed, the wounded party (or his or her pals) may retaliate with sabotage, spreading lies, poor performance appraisals, demotions, or firings. Retaliation is not just unfair; it produces legal liability.

- *They empty company coffers.*

A male manager sleeping with one of his staff is highly risky. Even if the affair seemed consensual, it might not have been entirely so (remember that last chapter), and the subordinate may sue for sexual harassment. Most cases settle out of court with millions of dollars wasted.

- *They create a sexualized environment.*

With sex in the air, employees may think personal comments and behavior are now okay. That can make other employees uncomfortable and opens the door to yet more legal liability.

- *They are especially bad for women.*

When a woman introduces her sexuality into the workplace, her co-workers see her in a different light, undermining her authority and professionalism. If the relationship ends badly, she is often negatively viewed and becomes the target of sexist gossip. If she decides to leave, moving quickly for personal reasons damages her career.

- *They can be crazy making.*

I once had to deal with a fist fight in the parking lot because of a warehouse romance gone wrong. Good grief.

- *The odds are against them.*

For every one that works out, hundreds don't. Romance in close quarters under constant scrutiny has little chance of survival. The stakes involving careers, paychecks, and professional aspirations are way too high to be subjected to the whims of the heart.

REAL LIFE

Here are some cringe-worthy examples I hope give you goose-bumps. First up is the married CEO who started an affair with the female COO. In this small company, word got around, and it made the employees nervous. What would happen if they broke up? The company's partners hated it and worried that confidential matters couldn't be discussed with either because of "pillow talk." The affair was indeed a sign of the end. When it dissolved, the company declared bankruptcy.

Then there was the guy who worked for me who began sleeping with a temporary administrative assistant. When she got pregnant, she quit. When the guy refused to marry her, she began calling all the senior leaders to pressure him to "do the right thing." That conversation was one of the worst I have had as a manager, especially when she broke down and cried.

Two friends of mine who worked closely together began hanging out, and love bloomed. They hid their affair for months. When they finally came clean to their boss, he became angry. Not just a little angry, but extremely angry. It damaged both of their careers. It's very hard to handle these situations well.

PROTESTATIONS

"I know someone who met the love of her life at work." "It happens all the time." "Some companies encourage dating between employees because then they spend more time at work." All those statements are true, but here are my thoughts about the counter arguments.

- ***It happens all the time.***
  This is true. It is astonishing how many workplace sexual encounters I've been privy to in my career. Bosses slept with secretaries; senior managers slept with each other; young people slept with everyone. Each case was peculiar

in its own horrible way, and almost none was good. Frequent practice doesn't mitigate risky behavior. People tailgate all the time—eventually with poor results. Office romances result in more damage than a crushed bumper; they cause crushed feelings, crushed careers, and crushed bank accounts. And, what if it happens all the time because we're not honest with employees about what a mistake it is? Perhaps we, as parents, mentors, managers, and leaders, should be more forthcoming about the damage office romance can wreak on a budding career.

- *You can't deny biology.*

This is another riff on the theme that men (and women, but mostly men) are a boiling pot of uncontrollable hormones, and if you put men and women together, they just can't help attacking each other like hyenas. I'm going to call BS on that one. If you think about that for a minute, I hope you'll agree that men and women refrain from having sex with each other in lots of situations. As an evolved human, you should be offended that someone thinks you have so little control of your actions.

- *What's wrong with a little love at the office?*

Hey, I'm all for love. I certainly did grow to love many of my colleagues. After years of working together, of getting to know their families, of caring for each other during tragic times, we did grow to love each other. But not all love has to be consummated sexually. And most of the sex I observed certainly wasn't love. It was sex.

- *We want people to have sex with their co-workers; that way they'll stay at the office and not go off to have a social life.*

This is the most offensive argument of all. To deliberately manipulate your employees and to encourage them to engage in unprofessional and damaging behavior for the alleged benefit of your bottom line makes me spit. Using your employees as sexual bait is reprehensible. Sex, affairs, and scandals will ensue. When it blows up in your face and you are sued for sexual misconduct, don't come crying to me.

- **But some people are happily married to people they met at work!**

This also is true. Given the number of office romances, there are bound to be one or two that work out. An office romance results in a spectrum of outcomes, from only-a-small-problem to a catastrophe, with many more on the catastrophe side. Office affairs are more likely to end badly, and we should be more upfront about that with our employees. We must explain how dangerous they can be, especially for women, to those we mentor. And, really? In the whole wide world, your soul mate just happened to be working in the same place as you? Uh-huh.

BETTER HUNTING GROUNDS

One friend who objected to Rule #1 asked where employees were supposed to go to meet potential mates if not at work. I hope you can see me rolling my eyes from there. Here are some possibilities I thought up in about five minutes:

At the gym, church, or salsa class; at Trivia Night, an astronomy lecture, or a Chris Isaak concert; at a Sierra Club hike, a Lego conference, or a laundromat; on an airplane or hot air balloon; at the dog park, the Smithsonian, or the old folks' home; at Comic-Con or open mic night; through friends, roommates, family, your alumni group, or French club; at a reunion, the emergency room, or a charity event; shoveling snow, wine tasting, or volunteering at the Christmas soup kitchen; at bingo, a fender bender, or a funeral; at a party, an AA meeting, a photography class, or a shoe store; playing softball or trick or treating; at the coffee house, the auto body shop, driving range, or shooting range; at a rally or a drone flying field; at a Go meeting or a bonsai growing workshop; at yoga or Burning Man; at your kid's school or the bowling alley; in line for ski tickets, the bluegrass festival, or beer; at an art gallery or a mud-wrestling contest; at a used bookstore, a car auction, or the Indy 500; and on the Santa Monica Pier. Oh, and online, which seems to have worked for thousands of happily married people.

Feel free to add your own. Someone who is looking for love on the job is suffering from a lack of imagination. And yes, you are supposed to have a life outside of work.

QUESTIONABLE COMPANY POLICY

In some states, the company has the option of formally forbidding employee relationships as a corporate policy. More and more companies are choosing this route because of the growing legal liability, albeit with the knowledge that realistically they aren't going to stop all relationships. I would be concerned that could create its own problems as some employees may find it titillating to flout company policy and be a part of the ensuing *scandale*. You certainly don't want to have to maintain a tip line where people can tell on each other. What would be next? Hiring private investigators and snooping around in someone's email? That all seems a bit over the top to me.

Some companies require the lovers to disclose their relationship, which strikes me as hard to enforce and even harder to interpret. Really? You're supposed to tell somebody at work about an uncomfortable one-night stand? That sounds invasive and kind of creepy. Other companies get those involved to sign an agreement, to say that the relationship won't affect their work and that it is consensual. I personally wouldn't want anything to do with that little signing party.

LINE IN THE SAND

I would, however, recommend your company's policy clearly forbids relationships between supervisors and subordinates. If such a relationship is reported or discovered, the supervisor must be fired, even if it was consensual. Note that it has to be applied across the organization no matter the rank of the supervisor. That means it applies to the CEO. That's when some companies lose their nerve about enforcing such rules.

I can hear you worrying about false accusations, but in my experience there were no gray areas. The relationship either existed or it didn't. I find that we worry sometimes about things that are unlikely to occur. That's not to say that you shouldn't think about what you'll do if someone denies an affair. People make messes, and it's up to the leadership to sort them out. It's helpful to have thought it through first.

In my view as a pragmatic manager, a company's policy should discourage romantic relationships between peers—but not forbid them. The policy should explain that office romances are bad for the company but also bad for employees. Managers and mentors should consistently follow up in their informal discussions with employees. Their approach should be, "It's not against the rules, but it's a bad idea, and here's why." Having everyone on board with Rule #1 will make your company a happy, civil place where men and women can work comfortably together and get a lot done.

MORE PRAGMATISM

And yet, it happens, right? As an individual, how do you deal with office romance? If it's outside your department or you're not a manager, you ignore it. As a professional, you should avoid getting involved in such a personal matter. Don't talk about the affair. Treat the parties involved with your usual respect and dispassion. If someone tries to draw you into the fray, you say, "That's their business, not mine."

NOT MY FAULT

Suppose a woman starts flirting with you at work? Quick answer: Shut that down. Just because she makes an overture doesn't make it okay. You must be the grown-up and bring your interactions back to a professional level. Don't try to blame her for something you did wrong just because she started it. If she persists, blame me— tell her you read a book about how you can't date women at work, not even one, no matter how much you might like to.

Be careful not to send the wrong signal. While I've encouraged you to socialize with your co-workers, some events are fraught with innuendo. One-on-one dinner and drinks, for example, might imply a more personal interest than you intended. A few times are fine, but making it a habit could be asking for trouble.

Alcohol also can cause an innocent situation to turn in a direction neither of you intended. Let me say that in a different way: Adding alcohol to an innocent situation can convert it into disaster. If you find yourself or your companion slipping down that slope, don't be a jerk and take advantage of the situation. Get out of there—alone.

Traveling together can also pose certain dangers that you didn't anticipate. It's unfortunate how often I hear about co-workers getting into trouble while abroad or at a conference. Late nights mixed with alcohol and forced closeness are a breeding ground for I-wish-I-hadn't-done-that's. What seems like a good idea at the time can turn out to be an extremely regrettable event in the cold light of day. If you're forewarned and alert, those sad stories won't happen to you. Keeping your wits about you can also help you keep a female colleague from making a mistake. A sensible person will appreciate you looking out for her.

THE EXCEPTION

Okay, what about if you are unlucky enough to fall in love with someone at work? Wait, have you been listening? Seriously, if you persist against all my sound advice, here's my advice about how to handle the situation so it does the least damage to you and to the company.

- *Tell no one.*
  People are incapable of keeping this kind of gossip secret. Make sure your paramour understands that. If she is the love of your life, she should get it.

- *Get out.*
  You must decide quickly who's going to leave the company because news of your relationship will leak. It's better for you both if that's after one of you has left.

ARE YOU SERIOUS?

In my casual conversations with friends and colleagues, most wom-en support Rule #1; it's the men who sometimes push back. Could it be that they resent the notion of a place where women are un-touchable? If men were nothing more than a seething bundle of uncontrolled hormones, I would be more sympathetic. But I know you are a rational being who knows better. If you are serious about creating a culture where women are happy and successful, you will accept the principle that they are not there for men to hit on.

Funny Ha Ha versus Funny Mean

Life would be tragic if it weren't funny.
~ Stephen Hawking

Think you're funny? Think again. Your female colleagues might not agree. Humor can bring a breath of fresh air to a work environment, but not when it makes women uncomfortable. I think some women should loosen up and not be so easily offended, but sometimes they are picking up on an undercurrent of ridicule or misogyny or resentment that has no place at work.

Some of the stories I've heard are bafflingly bad. Consider the poor woman whose co-worker threw dollar bills at her in appreciation of her hotness. She was appalled, but I suspect he didn't realize how insensitive his action was. He thought he was being funny. Yes, some men are that clueless.

EVERYBODY COULD USE A LAUGH

Humor can be a fabulous addition to your managerial skills, and work often is funny. Laughter is infectious and great medicine in the workplace. Humor can be a great tool to show humility, encourage a team, or smooth over a rough situation, but it must be used wisely with great sensitivity to the context and to the audience. The objective of humor in the workplace is to be inclusive and leave your co-workers with the sense that we are all in this together.

Some guys laugh at just about everything that sounds dirty, so be aware if you make a reference to an oral exam or a backdoor of any kind. That's not true for a lot of women. Besides not having much patience for eight-year-old humor, they have learned that men often joke at their expense and that their teasing can be cruel. Jokes that poke fun at women or leave women feeling left out are not effective. One of the most common ways men subtly harass women is with jokes that the men laugh at and the women don't.

"I'M JUST JOKING!"

Jokes about women are mostly not funny, and guys who tell them can have a nasty agenda. If someone must walk back their joke with the infamous excuse "I'm just joking," they have already lost credibility. That terrible phrase is also used to needle women about their apparent lack of a sense of humor, which only adds fuel to the fire. Men who have to use that line as a defense are on very weak ground.

SOME MEDIOCRE EXAMPLES

Q: Is Google male or female?
A: Female because it won't let you finish a sentence before making a suggestion.

Sure, it's kind of funny, but when the vast majority of jokes are about negative traits of women—they talk too much and don't listen; they drive badly; they're dumb; they won't have sex—you can see how jokes like this can get tiresome.

A guy I admired was trying to quiet a crowd, but they were too rowdy and kept talking. Finally, in frustration, he said, "I'm used to not being listened to—I'm married." That disappointed me. I think he really likes his wife and could have come up with something that was more clever and not the same old complaint about women. It wasn't just that *his* wife ignores him; the implication was that all wives ignore their husbands. Once again, the image of the overbearing, unsympathetic figure of the "wife" raises its head.

Who will laugh at this joke? Guys who are a little pissed off at their wives. Guys who think jokes about wives are funny. Guys who think jokes that make women look bad are funny. I don't think most wives will laugh at it. I didn't, and I'm pretty easygoing.

How about:

> *Q: What's the best way to find a truly committed man?*
> *A: Visit the closest mental hospital.*

Or

> *I have received hundreds of replies to my ad for a husband.*
> *They all say the same thing, "Take mine."*

Did you laugh? Maybe, but you can imagine how hearing hundreds of male-bashing jokes could turn hurtful and not amusing. Jokes that treat men as the enemy don't do much to improve gender relations.

BETTER ONES

Jokes about specific men and women can be funny, but these days women are on such high alert, I'd be careful about using gender-related humor, especially if it has a sexual overtone. What do you think about these?

> *A man was being arrested by a female police officer who informed him, "Anything you say can and will be held against you." The man replied, "Boobs!"*

Or

> *What did the elephant say to the naked man? "How do you breathe out of that thing?"*

Or

> *A husband and wife were having a fight and giving each other the silent treatment. The husband realized that he would need his wife to wake him the next day for an early morning flight. Not wanting to be the first to break the si-*

lence (and LOSE), he left a note on her side of the bed that read "Please wake me at 5 a.m." He awoke the next morning to discover that he had overslept. Furious, he was about to yell at her, when he discovered a note on his bedside table. It said, "It's 5 a.m. Wake up."

"SORRY, LADIES"

Guys, another sign that you're on shaky ground is when you have to apologize for your joke. This is doubly annoying to women because the implication is that the joke teller is really a gentleman (hence the apology), although the immediate evidence clearly demonstrates that he is not. And that he thinks "ladies" wouldn't find his joke funny. And that he doesn't understand how to use humor in the workplace.

GREAT ONES

I love jokes, and you can find some that I like on my website. Here are a few for you. After that last chapter, you probably need a laugh.

A guy asks his dumb friend to help him with something. "I think the blinker signal on my car may be broken. Can you stand behind the car and tell me if it's working?" The dumb guy says "Sure," and he goes behind the car. The other guy gets in the driver's seat and turns on the blinker signal. "Is it working?" he yells. "Yes!" says the dumb guy. "No! Yes! No! Yes! No!"

And

A guy has a talking dog. He brings it to a talent scout. "This dog can speak English," he claims to the unimpressed agent. "Okay, Sport," he says to his dog, "What's on the top of a house?" "Roof!" the dog replies. "Oh, jeez, come on . . ." the talent agent responds. "All dogs can say 'roof.'" "Wait," the guy says. He asks his dog, "What does sandpaper feel like?" "Rough!" the dog answers. The scout glares; he's losing his pa-

tience. "Hang on, hang on," says the guy. "This will amaze you," he says and turns to his dog and asks, "Who, in your opinion, is the greatest baseball player of all time?" "Ruth!" goes the dog, and the scout throws them both out of his office. On the street, the dog turns to the guy and says, "Maybe I should have said Derek Jeter?"

And

The government is sneaky. First they raise the tax on alcohol, then they make sure the country is such a mess that you drink more.

Okay, okay, back to serious business.

MALE BONDING

In December 2017, the *New York Times* asked 615 men about their behavior at work. Twenty-five percent said that they had told jokes or stories that some might consider sexist or offensive, made remarks that some might consider sexist or offensive, or displayed, used, or distributed materials (videos or cartoons) that some might consider sexist or suggestive. Men who admitted to telling sexual jokes or stories were five times more likely to report other behaviors such as unwanted stroking and pressing for a date after being told no.

Sexual jokes or general joshing about conquests or exploits present a common form of entertainment for guys at work, but they frequently make other people (men and women) uncomfortable. Anecdotally, I can report that many women find this behavior so objectionable that they bring it up again and again. The joking often carries a misogynistic undercurrent. When I was exposed to this kind of locker room talk, I felt there was often an effort to embarrass (and alienate) the women with side comments, like "How about you, Katherine? Do you and your boyfriend have that much fun?" Or to embarrass other men who didn't partake in the banter. "You plan on getting lucky tonight, Eduardo?"

Such behavior can create a climate in which routine harassment of the females is acceptable, but there are signs that company culture or leaders can have an effect in squashing it. The *New York Times* study indicated that harassing behaviors were prevalent among men who said their company didn't have harassment guidelines, their immediate supervisor didn't care about that kind of behavior, and no tip line existed to report complaints.

GATEWAY HUMOR

Even more problematic is when guys start acting as though the joking was all in fun but begin escalating the innuendo behind the jokes to the point it has turned into sexual harassment. Jokes about sex turn into questions about a woman's sexual behavior, followed by groping or touching.

NOT ONE OF THE BOYS

Those of us who see the danger in such behavior, either legally or because it results in a less happy workplace, have a responsibility to intervene. I found that a good tool for me was simply to walk away. It's hard to maintain sexual banter when you are alone. When someone starts talking dirty at work, one option for you is to just leave. You're saving yourself and the women around you.

If you are a manager of someone who is guilty of this behavior, you have to explain directly to him what sexual harassment is, how his behavior could be perceived as sexual harassment, and that it must stop. Put it in his performance appraisal. I know it won't be a comfortable conversation, but you picked up this book for a reason. Here's an opportunity for you to be a hero.

GOOD HUMOR

Effective humor in the workplace is inclusive, good-hearted, and smart. You would think that no one would be so insensitive as to joke about layoffs or corporate shake-ups, but, unfortunately, sometimes leaders get very confused and turn to gaiety to relieve themselves of the somber burden of communicating bad news. Kidding around about people's jobs or paychecks is completely inappropriate, and yet we see professionals make this mistake.

Sometimes you hear about an attempt at humor at work and you wonder *What were they thinking?* The problem is that they weren't. As humorists, we need to put ourselves in the shoes of our audience and mull through how the humor will come across. David Buss, an evolutionary psychologist, explained, "Humor signals a kind of ability to put yourself in someone else's mind and understand what someone else will find funny. It requires social intelligence, and it takes social verve or confidence."

WHO'S JOKING NOW?

Socially, men are usually the joke tellers, and it is more common for women to laugh at men's jokes than to tell jokes of their own. Setting aside the sexist view that women can't tell jokes, I suspect that dynamic is explained by the possibility that many men don't like to listen to women. Further, if a funny woman is a sign of a smart woman, she knows that's yet another mark against her. A writer researching this topic ran into the living room and asked her boyfriend if it was important to him that his sexual partners be funny. "Apparently not," he said. Ow.

Many women feel free to be funny as all get out—when men aren't around. As a test, you could set yourself a goal to see if you can get the women on your team to tell a joke. What a great way to tell if you've created an emancipated culture!

A HUMORFUL PLACE

It is fairly easy to avoid making mistakes with humor at work. Too often, we err on the side of avoiding humor because we are concerned about offending someone. It would be far better to apply these rules and take a chance. That said, mean jokes about women aren't funny. They're mean. And real gentlemen don't like to see women picked on.

You Look Nice

One frequently only finds out how really beautiful a woman is, until after considerable acquaintance with her.
~ Mark Twain

Guys ask me if they can comment on a woman's appearance, if that's still "allowed." In the distant past, my staff would occasionally compliment me on my appearance and then (judging by the look of horror that passed over their faces) have second thoughts about whether that was okay. So, it's a thing. Here are my two cents.

GIVE IT A REST

I'd avoid it. We talk too much about women's appearances as it is, from the time they are infants until they are grandmothers. If someone has clearly made an effort before a big presentation, you can say that she looks "professional" or "nice." Or if she has dressed up for the company's holiday party, you can say something complimentary, but don't pay undue attention to her appearance. She's not a spectacle for you to evaluate. There must be better things to discuss, especially at work. We know you're accustomed, if not required, to comment on a woman's appearance outside of work, but maybe we can make work a compliment-required free zone.

Okay, if she comes in with totally different hair, you're going to have to say something. Here's what you say: "Hey, you changed your hair. It looks great." That's it. Done.

NOT YOUR BUSINESS

Do you talk about a guy's appearance at work? Mostly not, unless you're kidding him about his bad haircut, his questionable beard, or his dirty shirt. Same rules apply for a woman. That goes for her appearance in general but especially such personal matters as her weight, her breasts, her legs, or her hairstyle. It's remarkable how shameless some men seem to feel in commenting about a woman's looks. If she didn't ask for your opinion, shut the hell up.

WHAT IF SHE DOES ASK?

Now you are entering murky waters. If you think she is fishing for a compliment, I wouldn't bite. I would either dodge the question or ask what she thinks. Then you can just agree with what she said and move on.

It's different if a staff member asks you if you think her appearance is appropriate for a special occasion. Unless her appearance is completely out of line, I would always answer the same way: "You look very nice." End of conversation. Don't get sucked into a larger conversation; if she asks again or for more reassurance or for more specifics, again say, "You look very nice." Isn't that easy? If you send a message that clothes, shoes, and accessories are much less important than how well prepared she is for the meeting, you have done her and the world a great service. We spend *way* too much money, energy, and yada yada on women's appearances. Now you can go back to work.

WELL...

If she is dressed in a way that would make a poor impression in that situation, you can counsel her to try something different next time. Emphasize that your suggestion isn't personal and that you're on her side; you want her to be well received and her appearance will be a factor. Explain that it's your opinion and you could be wrong. Make your comments dispassionate and explain that people have certain expectations. It's hard for people to swallow an unconventional appearance right off the bat. It's not wrong to surprise people, but it's better to do that *after* you've already made a good impression. That said, don't suggest to a woman that she wear make-up or dress in more feminine clothing. That's not her job, and I know you're not that dumb.

OOH LA LA!

In my book for executive women, I suggest that they don't dress provocatively at work. But despite my great advice, every year it seems women wear more and more revealing clothing—so that's a fact of work life right now. Men ask why women dress the way they do if they don't want the men to look. I don't have an answer—all I can say is, you can't look and you definitely can't touch. One wonders why someone who has so struggled to reach a professional level would undermine her own stature by wearing such girlish or sexy clothes, but so it is. They think they look nice.

WHAT IF SHE LOOKS BAD?

Surprisingly I hear most complaints about inappropriate dress from women who have strong opinions about what is acceptable. There is a lot to unpack here before you step into that cesspool.

First question up is if your company should have a dress code. Don't write a policy just because a few employees look like they should be at the beach (assuming that's not how everyone else dresses). The managers of those employees should intervene privately. The most important aspect of people's dress is their safety, such as wearing closed-toe shoes in the warehouse or safety glasses in a lab. But when women insist on wearing heels that are clearly an ankle-breaking threat, it's hard to write a decent policy. Perhaps you should do away with dress codes altogether. It's a quagmire fraught with hurt feelings, sexism, and gray areas. I personally like the idea of assuming your people will use their heads and dress accordingly.

If your leadership insists on a dress code, it should be general enough that it has wiggle room in case someone comes in wearing something the CEO objects to but wasn't specifically spelled out, like a backless dress. Terms like "business casual" or "appropriate for a professional office environment" are wooly and open to some interpretation, but that can be useful when you're writing a policy and not a law. Giving specific examples, such as "No flip-flops," is helpful. Note that there are legal requirements around accommodating religious or ethnic attire and grooming practices. It's always wise to get employees' input on the policy. If you have influence, though, don't let the company spend too much time on it. I've seen it take on a life of its own.

For our purposes here, the policy should be gender-neutral (in some states, it legally has to be). It shouldn't outlaw certain articles for women but not men, such as "Women cannot wear tank tops to the office." It shouldn't dictate requirements for women, but nothing equivalent for men, such as "two-to-four inch heels for women." I'd be careful in general about calling out rules for men and women separately. And good luck if you decide to take on the tattoos/piercings issue.

The thing is, what is the big deal about how women dress? I find there's hardly ever any controversy about what men wear, except maybe hats or holey jeans or dressing like a gang member. All our focus seems to be on the women, particularly if they are dressing like streetwalkers, or not dressing like women at all. Rather than regulating how women should dress, perhaps we should simply set a good example and expect them to figure it out. If a woman comes in frequently in attire that may affect her ability to be promoted or taken seriously, it's the job of the manager or coach to take her aside and advise her.

GOT SKILLS?

Ah. Suppose you are the unlucky person who has to do that job. How are you going to address such a sensitive topic? The same way you address all other difficult topics, such as bad breath, tardiness, nasty personal habits: You do it with courtesy, consideration, clarity, and calm.

As a good manager, you should broach a sensitive issue with sensitivity. You do it in private. You plainly state what the situation is. You ask for an explanation. You take appropriate action, whether it's requesting that she go home to change or recommending that she avoid that article of clothing in the future. Expect that she will be embarrassed and mad. Stay calm. Stand your ground.

Don't pass that job off on another woman and don't ever ask your admin to do it. And never mention it again.

A NEW APPROACH TO GIRLS

Outside of work, one strategy to change the world would be to follow the example of a friend of mine who made it a rule that she wouldn't talk about a girl's appearance anymore to her face. She noticed that she always unconsciously made a positive remark about how her young nieces looked when she visited them. Once she caught herself, she deliberately refrained from the you-look-nice comments. We may initially be at a loss for words, so accustomed are we to resorting to compliments about clothes or hair or accessories when talking to girls. It will take practice to come up with other ways of starting a conversation, but perhaps that effort will teach us to be more observant and personal, more focused on the individual girl herself. Telling girls that their appearance is not the most important thing about them, and then proving it by talking about something else is a two-pronged strategy that could counteract society's constant focus on their looks. It's worth a try.

Awkward Moments

He stared for ten seconds or more, which,
when eating a chocolate cake isn't much, but when staring, is.
~ Louise Penny

I hate to break it to you, but other topics besides appearance can make employees and managers uncomfortable. Intensely private matters can arise at work. We may be able to stumble our way through them when we are of the same gender, but discussing sensitive issues with someone of the opposite sex whom we don't know well—it's not for the faint of heart.

BE DISCREET

When both sides are well-intentioned, we can deal with personal matters with discretion, kindness, and dispassion. Women may be very reluctant to discuss personal female matters, like pregnancy, menstruation, or medical issues. Please grow some common sense and don't press for information that isn't your business. Just as talking about a guy's prostate or hemorrhoids could be terribly embarrassing, so it might be for her. In polite society, we are discreet about such matters, and the workplace should be no exception.

Also, there's no reason to share what you know with other employees. What a faux pas. And yet, I've heard supervisors toss off some cruel comment about a woman's private matter for the amusement of his buddies. When the woman finds out, it's really horrifying to see her cringe with humiliation. Of course, you would never do that. What was I thinking.

WATCH IT WITH THE TOUCHY-FEELY

It is staggering how many complaints I hear about men touching women at work. Is it really that hard to keep hands off? Men are sometimes sending a proprietary and disrespectful message about women's bodies when they engage in casual touching. It would be easy to say just never touch women you work with, but sometimes it is natural and kind to touch someone's arm, or give them a hug, or put your arm around someone. But it shouldn't be frequent and it shouldn't be icky. Also don't be stupid. If someone tells you not to touch her or shrugs your hand off, pay attention. You're making her uncomfortable.

TEARS

I've long suspected that one of the reasons men don't want to work with women is because women cry. I counsel my clients to never cry in the workplace, but it happens all the time. I was floored by how frequently women cried at work. If a woman cries in your office, first don't freak out. It might not be a big deal. Most women haven't been coached to "*never* cry" since they were five, as perhaps you were.

Consider also that her tears may not signify sadness; she might be angry or exasperated, and those emotions may come out in liquid form. I sometimes wonder if women have been taught not to yell, and so they cry, and if men have been taught not to cry, and so they yell. In any case, don't run away from her when she cries. Give her a tissue and ask her what's going on. Your calm will help her recover from the embarrassment of crying and allow you both to move on to better communication and problem-solving.

THE MANIPULATOR

So far you're doing great, right? Anybody can work with women! Just use your head, act like a reasonable person, and you're fine.

And then a woman throws a spanner in the works. I've made it look easy because you've only had to deal with hypothetical women. If we raise the bar and let in some real-life women, you are going to have to handle some tougher situations.

What if a woman implies that she has private matters that she can't talk about? Oh boy. Don't think that all women are above pulling these shenanigans. If someone detects that there are topics that make you so uncomfortable you run in the other direction, she can use that to her benefit. Some women presume that a guy wouldn't be willing to call them on such manipulative behavior and abuse that power. Keep your head and don't get thrown off your game.

On the other hand, you want to avoid getting drawn into the personal lives of your female employees. The rule holds for male employees also, but some women are less protective of their private lives than they should be. You don't want employees pouring out their hearts to you, and you don't want to get involved to the extent that your judgment is clouded or you start giving someone special treatment because of their personal situation. The guys in your group will pick up on that in a heartbeat and it will piss them off. Working with women doesn't mean letting them walk all over you.

FAIRNESS

In navigating the workplace, it is impossible to always be completely fair. Life is complicated. You are trying to create as fair an environment for your female employees as you can, with sensitivity to ways she might face special challenges. You try to apply the rules objectively to both men and women, and you attempt to treat them the same. That's the ideal, at least.

It is not easy, and you may catch yourself criticizing or making allowances for certain employees because of their gender, their age, their background, or their personal circumstances. When you catch yourself or someone calls you out on it, you should acknowledge your mistake and remedy it. But don't beat yourself up. It's really hard to overcome biases that have been instilled in you since you were young. You're trying to do the right thing, which under these conditions is a difficult thing. Good for you for trying.

What's Wrong with Her?

I'm not bad. I'm just drawn that way.
~ Jessica Rabbit

In the last chapter, I raised the specter of the manipulative, less-than-perfect female co-worker. I can imagine your shock. News flash! Not all women in the workplace are fun to work with. I'll bet you've run across a few. I've heard people say about someone, "What's **wrong** with her?" I won't lie. Sometimes something is wrong with her. Let's dive in.

ANY ADVICE ABOUT WORKING WITH WOMEN?

When my first book came out, I noticed a common reaction. The book is titled *The Discreet Guide for Executive Women: How to Work Well with Men (and Other Difficulties)*, which sounds hostile to men although the book isn't. Women would read the title, chuckle, tell me about some awful male boss or co-worker and then say—wait for it—"Actually, I think women are harder to work with than men." It usually took them less than two minutes before (since we just don't have enough stories about how women can't get along) here would come another. Very often, they reported that women they worked with "held them back," "weren't supportive," "were psychos at work," or "stabbed me in the back." I was struck by the common language they used, particularly the searing "I thought she was my friend."

Then people started writing me to ask if I had any advice about working with women. "Any advice about working with a female boss?" a new reader wrote. "Do you have anything about other women?" another wrote desperately. It got so bad I thought somebody better write the book, *The Indiscreet Guide to Working with Women (and Other Impossibilities)*.

Joking aside, the anecdotes and statistics are not fun. According to various surveys, most employees prefer male mentors and male bosses. Many of the women I mentor report problems, not with their male colleagues, but with their female ones. Some of these stories are really disturbing. It's a rare guy who will openly say that he had trouble working with a woman. If he knows me well, he'll mention it, usually with consternation—like What was *wrong* with her? Many guys will stoutly say that they worked for a woman, and they had *no* problem with that. That's in public, so to speak. The anonymous reports tell a different story. People complain about a woman's inability to communicate, to take a joke, to join in, to be a team member. These reports make me so sad—after a good five decades of women in the workforce, this is where we are?

THE ELEPHANT IN THE ROOM

The American Bar Association published a survey showing that legal secretaries did not prefer to work for female partners over male partners, which provoked a ferocious backlash from women's groups. The association said the survey revealed the "elephant in the room" that "we don't allow ourselves to talk about." Then people got really mad. The leadership of the association finally threw up their hands and apologized and scheduled some town hall sessions on gender equality.

Meanwhile, another reader politely wrote to me, "Interactions with female colleagues would also be a useful topic to cover." And a young woman wrote sadly, "In my area, I find that other women are like obstacles, but I suppose this would be the case anywhere."

SOME GIRLS ARE "BETTER" THAN OTHERS

As the English rock band the Smiths previously observed, not all women are alike. Imagine a grim, uptight, paranoid colleague who takes everything the wrong way. She's ready to pull herself up in outrage at every imagined slight. She's stiff, hostile, and carries a giant chip on her shoulder. She's insecure about her competence, so she doesn't ask or answer questions, overuses lingo in an attempt to fit in, and hides behind inauthentic emails and overly formal presentations. She barricades herself in her office and discourages drop-in visits. Wow. I bet you want to build a relationship with her, right?

People don't want to build a relationship with this unpleasant person. And I hear awful reports of her continued existence from all corners and of the damage that she wreaks on careers and staff members' mental health. Nevertheless, at the risk of infuriating everyone—those stung by a female co-worker and the elephant-deniers—I'm going to stick up for those Not-So-Good Women. When I hear about a witch at work, I think about how miserable and confused she must feel.

A DODGE

In my first book, I consciously didn't include stories about nasty women; after all, I coached my readers to be kind to women at all levels of the organization and not to diss female public figures. A fellow senior executive commented disapprovingly, "Well, that *is* quite a dodge." In my defense, I did it because I think the way to fix that problem is to fix those women; in my view, almost all that bad behavior stems from insecurity, unhappiness, and desperation in the workplace. We need to make these women feel better, so that they can perform effectively and deal with their leaders, colleagues, and subordinates in a supportive and correct way.

DEEP BREATH

I'm going to ask you for a bit of sympathy for this flawed employee. When she's been the underdog, when she's had to fight for the right to play, when she's been spit on by the crowd through every match she's played, and when even her own teammates subtly undercut her, she's likely to be pretty pissed, and accidents are gonna happen. Because of inexperience, new rules, and clumsiness, it's very hard for her to play a clean game. She's going to commit some fouls, and the ref is going to make some harsh calls.

But the women are coming along, and they're getting better. They're out on the playing field where no women played before. They're playing a men's game, and the men are letting them play. We're all figuring it out, so let's not give up on them yet.

THE TAKEAWAYS

A bit of sympathy doesn't mean that those Not-So-Good-Women don't have to come around eventually. I'm not asking that you change the rules for them. We still want employees to behave at work, to be cordial to their co-workers, to be good team members, and to obey the rules of appropriate work behavior. But I am asking you to give them a chance. They may need some extra mentoring, coaching, and training. These confused employees may require some time before they realize you want them to succeed.

The other takeaway is that you can't rely on other women to mentor and develop your female employees. Lots of guys would love to push the responsibility for their female employees off onto someone else, but they do that at their peril. In those organizations, managing and mentoring of the junior female employees seem to fall between the cracks, resulting in little improvement and in a poor experience for them. Now that you're aware of this pitfall, that won't happen at your company. You and the other male employers must consciously take on that responsibility. So, sorry, it's still up to you.

Test Your Company for Sexism

I believe most people are essentially good. I know that I am.
It's you I'm not entirely sure of.
~ Stephen King, *Full Dark, No Stars*

Just as individuals can engage in routine discrimination without realizing it, so can companies. Companies may be even more susceptible because they have no self-awareness. Here are some ideas for you to consider as you evaluate how fair your company is to women.

EQUAL PAY FOR EQUAL WORK

I discovered pay discrimination in my company by happenstance. I was working as a mid-level finance manager for a company that I thought was very well run. I undertook some payroll analysis and discovered that in every job category, *every* female was paid less than *any* man. There was no classification in which a woman made more than a man. It was as though two pay scales existed for every job category. In addition, the most senior positions were held exclusively by men. I wasn't surprised by the latter fact; I was astounded by the first.

You, too, can run this exercise on your own if you have access to the data, or with the cooperation of the senior management team. It's just facts after all. But facts can tell a lot about the attitudes of managers who control compensation. It might not be deliberate, in fact, I would doubt that it is, but if your company turns out to be like mine, it's engaging in discrimination.

HOW COULD THIS HAPPEN?

Don't underestimate the power of early subtle differences in pay. If a woman comes in earning slightly less than her male equivalent and then gradually receives slightly lower pay adjustments, it can result in a big pay gap after a few years. If this gets amplified across the company, you'll end up with a situation like mine, where every job category reveals a gender pay gap. It wasn't done on purpose, but it's what can happen when you're not paying attention. As with all subtle acts of discrimination, you must actively watch for small actions that result in a big problem.

Women can be complicit in this effect despite my constant coaching that they need to advocate for themselves. Over the course of my career, on several occasions I have had to question why no salary adjustment was being made for a woman at year-end when increases were given to men in the same department. If they haven't heard otherwise, even human resource professionals assume that a woman is satisfied with her salary. Under my questioning, they would say in surprise, "Oh, she's happy." How did they know she was happy? "Well, she hasn't said anything."

Much has been written about women and negotiating, and some excellent books are available about this interesting topic. I'll summarize the findings for you: Many women hesitate to negotiate, they don't do it very well, and they are frequently criticized when they try. As a result, compared to guys, they may start with lower salaries, get smaller bumps when they get promoted, and receive fewer bonuses.

You will have to listen hard to see if your colleagues express irritation with a woman who negotiates. If they don't express equal frustration with a guy who negotiates, you are observing bias in action. Sometimes a woman who asks for more is seen as ungrateful or whiny while a negotiating guy is perceived to be standing up for himself and recognizing his self-worth. Those attitudes will result in a culture that is not welcoming to women who *do* know their self-worth. Strong-minded women who know their market value will negotiate a better salary at another company and leave. You may have saved yourself a few thousand dollars, but you'll have lost a valuable resource: a high-quality, assertive employee.

If you are in a position to mentor or manage women, be sure to coach them about good ways to negotiate. They should come in with facts, competitive salary range information, and impartial analysis of the duties of the job they perform, not arguments that are based on loyalty or personal efforts. Companies pay for the job, not the person. Sometimes women don't understand that intuitively, and so their arguments for why they should be paid a certain amount don't carry the day.

THINGS THAT DON'T WORK

I have to address some nonsense here. In California, a law has recently gone into effect that prohibits employers from asking candidates about their salary history. This supposedly well-intentioned law was meant to halt the proliferation of the gender pay gap. It was assumed that a company would offer the same pay to candidates of either gender for the same job if they didn't know that the woman had made less than the man in their previous jobs. Given what you know about gender bias and women's difficulty with negotiating, you can see this won't work. The company will offer the woman less because it doesn't value her as highly, and she won't negotiate as hard as the guy will because she doesn't have a realistic view of her worth—and she knows it will be poorly viewed if she attempts to negotiate. And we are back to square one.

To add insult to injury, the law doesn't prohibit companies from accepting salary history information if candidates offer it up. Nor are companies prohibited from asking what the candidates' expectations are. So guess who is more likely to provide that information since she wants to be helpful? This law could end up worsening the pay gap when companies know what the women made but not the men.

Can we talk about your brain for a moment? Across the nation, proposals like this come forth which sound good and people mindlessly sign on without thinking through the consequences. If you are a true friend to women, you will be cautious about jumping on your company's politically correct band wagon when issues come forth that create a false appearance of gender equality but don't really help women.

Another silly idea is for companies to proclaim that they don't negotiate hiring salaries. This sounds good until you think about it for one minute. Of course, companies *will* end up negotiating in a tight job market. If they don't negotiate the base salaries, they will negotiate vacation, stock options, signing bonuses, and myriad other perks. Under enough pressure from candidates and hiring managers, they will negotiate base salaries too. That policy is doomed to be a lie. It's also doomed to work against women. Some women will be fooled into thinking that the hiring salaries aren't negotiable (and obey the "rules") while aggressive guys will test the waters to see what is negotiable. Again, the ones who advocate effectively for themselves win.

Your company should undertake a good analysis of what each position entails, what it is worth on the open market and whether an additional skill or certification would justify a difference in pay. Frequent analysis by gender of your positions and what employees in those positions are earning will help pinpoint cases where the pay gap has inserted itself. Gender bias is so insidious that you have to be vigilant to snuff it out before it's gone viral and its effects are felt everywhere.

PERFORMANCE APPRAISALS

Good evaluation forms include quantitative assessments that measure successful completion of routine tasks and annual goals. The appraisals should be closely tied to year-end salary increases. Using numeric measurements will help women (and men who might otherwise be discriminated against). Sure, a manager might err on the side of a lower score for a woman, but if total raw scores are equal between a man and a woman, it's harder to excuse a smaller increase for the woman.

THINGS THAT DO AND DON'T MATTER

Companies try to sell themselves as female friendly with various bits of special policies. They point to maternity benefits, flexible schedules, childcare, and coverage of family planning services. I get that they are trying to present certain aesthetics to appeal to women, but these worry me if they make men or childless women feel bad. I personally would question policies that blatantly favor women (or anyone based on their gender), but I'm probably a lone wolf crying in the wild. I tell my clients their salary, bonuses, and potential for promotion are what matter. The rest is window dressing.

Statistics will help you perform a real test of your company. Take a look at the profile of your company: What percentage of women are in various departments and in the company overall? While you're at it, check for diversity in general. Do you have a mix of young and old people? People of different colors? People of different sizes? Liberals and conservatives? Does the diversity hold up department by department? I'm not a fan of quotas, but we tend to hire people who look like we do, so we may not notice when we've created a department of young male Purdue grads or liberal private-school-educated women. Someone else would notice though.

Other considerations should go into the mix. Do you have a history of sexual harassment lawsuits or complaints? What is the outcome of those disagreements? What is turnover like for men compared to women? Do women rise to a certain level and then walk out? What information is coming out of your exit interviews? If you have special programs to hire and retain women, how are they working?

THE FACE OF YOUR COMPANY

I tell women to ignore whatever is said in interviews about whether the company is friendly to women. Someone has been told to say those things, and they mean nothing. I do coach them to evaluate a potential employer in several ways: Are there women in upper management and on the board? It's not a perfect test, but it's a start. So, for you, make sure you have some women in high places.

At this point, dang it, having an all-white, all-male senior management team and board of directors is simply inexcusable. And don't just stick some woman in human resources and call it good. Give a meaty job to a woman.

INSIDE BASEBALL

Once women are on the inside, they probably have opinions about how women are treated at your company. They may not tell you until they feel safe and protected from retaliation. If you have an internal women's network or group, you can visit or hang out and see what they say. Not everything that women complain about is valid, but you may hear some tales that you would never have known about otherwise.

I went to speak at a local large tech company about gender issues. We anticipated about forty people. The large room quickly overflowed, and dozens of people lined up in the hallway outside. The women in attendance were *wound up* and intent on being heard. The energy in the room was palpable. They wanted to express their frustration with being dissed, not taken seriously, not listened to—and paid less than their male counterparts. They were not shy; they finally had an outlet to vent. Does your company provide a forum to hear from women or other minorities?

Participating in women's groups or conferences on the outside can also be helpful to understand what their challenges are, learn how they talk when men aren't around, and build your network of highly capable, high-quality women. Extra credit if you bring along a work buddy. If no one will go with you, well, what can I say. Eventually one hopes such groups won't be needed, but they sure are now.

SPECIAL PROTECTION FOR ADMINS

Here here for admins. These souls are often carrying tremendous responsibilities, are knowledgeable about your company, and work very hard for little pay and little acknowledgment. One good way to ensure that you're working for a good company is to confirm with the admins that they are treated well. I advise building a strong relationship with all the admins—treat them with respect, listen to their wise advice, and be thankful if you yourself have a good one.

TRASH-TALKING

Throughout my career, I've hated it when men made sexist remarks about women. "Women can't get along." "Women never notice what kind of plane they're flying in." "Women can't read maps." It bugged me because there's so much variability among women that exceptions to these generalizations can always be found. Not to mention that they were often demeaning. For heaven's sakes, some women are pilots—you think they don't notice what kind of plane they're flying?

It also used to irk me when women would make sexist remarks about men. "Men can't multitask." "All they think about is sex." "Men can't handle pain." Ah, hang on a sec. I can think of a few guys who have handled pain. I don't like this trash-talking about the opposite sex, and I think those stereotypes are inaccurate and misleading.

This is a good opportunity for you to open your ears to listen for these foolish generalizations in your workplace. I'll leave it to you to decide if you're going to speak up when you hear them, but it's good practice to note it to yourself at a minimum. If you hear a lot of this kind of talk among your male peers, you know who you're dealing with and what you're up against to transform that into a positive environment for women.

BULLIES

Bullies flourish in toxic workplaces, and they tend to target women. These insecure men try to get their way by force and intimidation. They use their body and their voice in a threatening manner to cow other employees. They're quick to anger and have found that yelling and threatening are effective tools in the workplace. In my experience they often aren't very bright and suffer from a lack of emotional intelligence. When they're outgunned intellectually or verbally, they resort to bullying to gain a superior position. They tend to be emotional and unhappy.

Some men bully "down" an organization; they focus on people who are lower on the totem pole. Many men prefer to bully women because they think they won't fight back, and such targeted bullying can evolve into sexual harassment or discrimination. I coach women about how to handle bullies, but I can't be on-site everywhere. You can give me a hand if you observe it happening in your workplace. I'll leave it to you how to best intervene, but intervene you must. Recognize that your company will be better if it doesn't tolerate such poor behavior and mistreatment of its employees.

A cautionary word here: Bullying is a real thing, but over the past few years, it's become a word casually thrown around for any kind of conflict. You'll have to use your head when someone comes to you with a complaint of bullying. Accusing someone of bullying is not the same as proving it. Fighting, criticizing, or arguing aren't the same as bullying. Bullying requires a pattern of behavior in which someone uses their rank, size, or power to gain an unfair advantage. A mean warehouse manager who intimidates someone into routinely giving up their lunch hour is a bully. A loud guy who lost his temper in a meeting and yelled at a peer isn't a bully. He can be chastised for losing control, but he shouldn't be labeled with that particular b-word.

WOMAN-HATERS

Have you ever encountered someone who seemed to have it out for all women? Some people always seem to have a disparaging comment ready for a woman. They think the worst of her behavior, habits, intentions, and motivations. There's real venom behind their attitude that appears uncalled for. You may be in the presence of a woman-hater. They come in both male and female forms and are more common than you may think. Identifying them is useful so you can put their accusations in perspective if they complain about a woman.

Sadly, there are a lot of man-haters, too, but you will encounter fewer of them if you work in a company dominated by men. Man-hating is a blood sport for some women, and you have my sympathy if you uncover much of such unpleasantness.

HOW DID IT GO?

Did your company fare well when considered under a microscope? I hope so. Many companies are working hard to welcome a diverse population of employees. It is surprising however how many companies are blissfully unaware of their obvious discrimination as proven by the faces of their leadership, their salary structures, and the unhappiness of their employees.

Good Good Good Management

Accept the fact that we have to treat almost anybody as a volunteer.
~ Peter F. Drucker

Warning, detour ahead. Stay with me while I shift gears and change the subject for a minute. While I have you (sort of) captive, here are some fundamental management basics that I believe should be practiced far and wide. They apply to both your male and female subordinates. In my work, I encounter so many stories of terrible managers that I have to stick my oar in whenever I can. It's frustrating that for as long as we have known about good management principles and what good management looks like, we still have such god-awful managers out there. I'll be brief and use short words.

PURE GOLD

Your employees are your most important assets. Really. I found that loyal, hardworking, knowledgeable employees were almost always undervalued, particularly by senior leaders who came and went. Those long-term employees make a company what it is. How ironic that accounting principles require you to put all kinds of nonsense on your balance sheet, and those extremely valuable employees don't show up. But you and I know that if they leave, you are toast.

Also how heartbreaking it is that they are often mistreated. But not by you, right?

YOUR RESPONSIBILITY

When your company gives you supervisory authority over other human beings, it is trusting you to not screw up their lives. You must care for those individuals, pay attention, and provide resources, support, and a sympathetic ear. You must create a nurturing environment for them. You must ensure they are appropriately compensated, and that they receive **training** for their shortcomings. You are now responsible for those individuals' professional success. It is up to you to ensure that they gain skills, advance in their career, and are ready for each challenge they will face. Their resume should look better after they leave you than it did when they came to you.

Sounds hard, right? You bet. People management is the most difficult part of your job because nothing is more complicated than people messing around with other people. But it can be the most rewarding if you do it right.

THE TRADE

You must collaborate with your subordinates, and that will require humility on your part. You must acknowledge that you know less than they do—about their job, their situation, their frustrations. That's why you listen to and learn from them. You provide access to resources and get them help so they can perform their duties. In exchange, if you've done that part right, they help you. They work toward your team's goals, and you all get a lot of good work done, culminating in your company's success.

COMPANY INTEREST VERSUS SELF-INTEREST

You're also responsible for coaching your employees about how to advocate for themselves. Don't let the company take advantage of someone who is in your care. Explain how to make an effective argument, and demonstrate it for them. Communicate the basics of negotiation and how to do so in good faith. Explain ethical, fair behavior and what it means to be a team player. Show how each employee must work for the common good but not at the detriment of his or her self-interest. Make clear that the company's success will translate to personal success.

WORK ON YOURSELF

Good management is hard work. Get all the training you can for difficult conversations, interviewing, conflict management, dealing with poor performers, and terminations. Learn not to undermine, abuse, ridicule, blame, belittle, or yell at your staff. Then practice. It's stunning how much we require of our managers—then offer little training and never have them practice. Firing someone is one of the most difficult tasks we face in our professional lives, and we rarely practice beforehand.

HIRE WELL

Write a job description with a list of required, bona fide qualifications. Don't use pointless qualifications as a screening device. Advertise widely. Offer an attention-getting bonus for referrals from existing employees. Take your time. Build a pool of candidates. Form a hiring committee of people with different perspectives. Don't let one influential person hijack the process. Let the recruiter's voice be just one of many. Accept internal candidates with grace, appreciation, and an open mind. Use tests or quantitative measures to assess skill. Forget personality tests. Ask questions relevant to the job; don't ask stupid brain-teaser questions. Hire people with proper qualifications; don't just hire someone who seems talented, and say you'll figure out what they do later. Ignore how they dress or what they drive. Take credentials with a grain of salt. Ask around about the person. Don't ignore red flags. Run a transparent process. Don't hire anyone who lies on their resume— that includes omissions. Try not to hire relatives. Don't give jobs as favors. Don't use quotas. Treat all candidates with respect. Notify and thank candidates who were not selected. After all the input is in, the hiring manager gets to (and has to) make (and own) the decision. If you end up with a bad hire, admit it, and review what went wrong during the hiring process.

MAKING MANAGERS

Don't put people with bad people skills in charge of other people. It's evil.

POLITICS

It is terribly common for organizations to hire a good person and then have them report to an inappropriate person, such as someone in a different department. The poor employee is put in a no-win position as their manager can't protect or support them, understand their problems, or control their daily surroundings. Bad companies hand out supervisory responsibilities like treats, sacrificing good employees and sowing chaos.

CLEAR AUTHORITY

Each job position should have a sensible title, a written set of responsibilities, and one solid reporting line to an internal boss. Dotted lines are BS. The boss must have responsibility for writing each subordinate's performance appraisal, determining their salary (inside a range), and assigning their day-to-day tasks. If even one of the three is missing, the relationship is destined to suffer.

MEETINGS

Have few committees and few group meetings. Require agendas. The discussion must stay on topic. Avoid "round-robin" reporting that is stupor-inducing and encourages self-promotion. Focus on decision-making and action. Start and end on time. Latecomers have to sit in the back. Those who use excessive business jargon are put in a time-out. Minutes are taken and distributed. The role of minute taker rotates. Participation, dissenting or harmonious, is encouraged, as are food and laughter.

INTERVENTION

Conflict is inevitable, and it's not all bad. When strong-minded individuals disagree and make their arguments well and productively, we have better outcomes. When snarky, unspoken, stab-you-in-the-back conflict arises, don't ignore it. Address it while it's still a small problem and before things go pear-shaped. Many managers try to dodge unpleasant incidents, but they tend to fester instead of going away. If someone is rude, attacks someone by email, or otherwise misbehaves, don't let that go. You can wait a day or so until everyone calms down, but it's your job to keep your employees working well together in a respectful way. That's why you're paid the big bucks.

If you and human resources aren't making progress, get coaching, training, and mediation early and use them liberally. Adopt the attitude that help from the outside is beneficial and will work. Unresolved conflict is destructive and all too common. It moves around a department or company like a virus and sickens innocent bystanders. And it can be very expensive if it results in a lawsuit.

RESPECT AND HONESTY

Be honest with your employees. That's how you build trust. You can't tell them everything you know, but be up front about that. Say "I can't talk about that" and explain why. Don't lie, and don't spin. Employees smell that, and then they want to smack you. Remember that you are fiddling with their livelihood when you hide things. Be careful. Employees, even low-level employees, think a lot more about the company, how it's run, and what its prospects are than most managers realize.

Good managers talk to their employees and listen. Most managers don't meet as frequently with their employees as they should, and bad managers ignore their staff. Time spent together creates a strong partnership that can be a source of great satisfaction in your work life. Your subordinates also may have excellent ideas because of their experience and position. The value of diversity comes from different perspectives, no matter what color or gender they're wrapped in.

A MANAGEMENT GEM

Each employee should write a monthly report and meet with their manager to discuss it. In bullet point format and limited to one page, it presents the accomplishments of the month and the goals for the next. Monthly monitoring will keep annual goals on track. When items remain "stuck" in the goals section month after month, they can be used to uncover roadblocks or unveil procrastination. If appropriate, they can be broken down into smaller more manageable items, or removed if they are no longer important or relevant. The manager can also review the subordinate's subordinates' reports at the same time to be sure the whole team is moving in the same direction. That way, the manager ensures that the subordinate is meeting with his or her subordinates and taking care of them, and the whole wonderful loop is closed.

The meeting provides an opportunity for informal positive and negative feedback about how things went during the past month. The manager can note that feedback in the margins of the report before filing it. Suggestions for improvements can be provided without the sting of a formal performance appraisal. Misunderstandings don't fester. If something is bugging either party, the one-on-one meeting is the time to get it out. At the time of performance evaluation, the manager pulls out twelve monthly reports and, voilà, the annual appraisal practically writes itself. The full year is visible, and more recent issues don't unduly influence the overall report.

PERFORMANCE APPRAISALS

Do them with care and on time. It sends a horrible message to your subordinates when you can't even spare the time or energy to discuss with them how they are doing at their jobs. Quantitative assessments help eliminate bias in performance assessment and salary increases. Appraisals should evaluate the completion of both routine job responsibilities and annual goals. It's fair to include issues such as rudeness to co-workers, hostility, insubordination, and poor attitudes. The forms should be no more than three pages long. They shouldn't include a bunch of buzz words and nonsense. Before being sent upstairs, written performance appraisals should be personally reviewed and discussed with employees (like civilized human beings).

TROUBLEMAKERS

Start first with the real conviction that you can help troublemakers find healthier ways to behave at work. If you are worried about someone, seek to understand and offer support. Try to surround your potential troublemaker with people whom they can trust and who will be able to advise them about reality.

I have found that some women hold incredibly naïve ideas about how an organization works, what amount of power they have the right to exercise, and how fast they can reasonably expect to progress. When people feel powerless and trapped, bad things can happen. All of this can and should be explained by experienced people who can help them understand how companies operate. It may still all go sideways and you'll end up getting rid of them, but women's complaints at work frequently have some truth behind them even if they aren't quite as they were initially presented.

PERFORMANCE IMPROVEMENT

One of the most common complaints employees have is that their employer won't deal with poor performers. When you take action to improve someone's performance, you are doing so on behalf of the employee, yourself, your company, and other employees. Don't hide someone's shortcomings from them. This is such a common and surprising problem. Sometimes everyone on the senior leadership team knows something about someone—that she nitpicks her employees to death or he has a temper problem—and yet no one has told the employee. That is the manager's fault.

Performance problems should be addressed in person and documented in writing. Dates of meetings should be noted with a predetermined time for a follow-up meeting. Don't skip follow-up meetings. Employees need to know how they are doing. If another incident occurs before the next follow-up, an immediate meeting should be held. If the problem merits it, the employee should be told that a lack of improvement will result in termination.

Communicate that you are on their side, and explain why the company must see a change. Employees go through ups and downs. Give them a real chance to remedy a problem. Protect them if someone else is victimizing them. Don't fire someone just because someone powerful doesn't like them.

TERMINATIONS

If there is a lack of improvement, the employee must be fired, no matter how much others try to interfere or nervous attorneys shriek. The termination needs to be supported by good documentation and clear communication. There must be due process which follows company policy. Don't fire someone because of public pressure; you can expect a lawsuit if you do (Hey there, Google). Assume everyone is watching, but don't talk to other employees about the situation. Don't use the "we're eliminating your position" tactic to get rid of someone. It hamstrings your organization to hire properly afterward, and everyone knows it's baloney. The most frequent cause of termination is absenteeism. If someone isn't coming to work, you have to decide how much leeway you are willing to give, based on longevity or the situation. Be clear about your expectations and follow up accordingly.

Be deliberate leading up to the event, but make the execution speedy. Be respectful and regretful. Say you're sorry it didn't work out. Thank them for their service. Focus on facts. Don't make it personal. Just talk; don't hide behind formalities. I was once let go while I was overseas by someone reading a long legal document over a phone with a bad connection. I kept having to yell "What?" during this meaningless ordeal. Talk about awkward. Don't have security walk them out. Notify other employees about the departure. Lastly, don't bad-mouth the employee afterward. There but for fortune go you.

LAYOFFS

A reduction in force is a terrible, inhumane atrocity wreaked on innocent employees by careless or incompetent senior management.

I recognize I'm an outlier here, but I find the modern era of frenzied hiring and subsequent layoffs has given rise to a really callous attitude toward turning someone's life upside down. Do anything to avoid a layoff. If it must happen, beat yourself and the management team up about it, learn from it, and never let it happen again.

VOLUNTARY DEPARTURES

An unsurpassed opportunity to solicit honest input about your company presents itself with the exit interview, when an employee voluntarily leaves the company. Don't miss out on their feedback. This information should be carefully preserved and analyzed. Turnover is expensive, damages morale, and reflects poorly on your company.

GO FORTH

Thanks for reading. Now that you have been indoctrinated, I hope you join my quest to spread those important principles across all organizations and make our workplaces better. Here we are, you and I, doing our part to improve the world and the working lives of people everywhere. Now back to our regularly scheduled programming.

What the World Needs Now . . .

Just do right. . . .
Take up the battle. . . .
It's yours. This is your life.
This is your world.
~ Maya Angelou

We are nearly finished. I'll end with a request. And a caution.

STAND UP FOR WOMEN!

I've saved the best for last. If more men were to speak up on behalf of women, we would see a dramatic decline in their mistreatment at work. When you see anyone being hurt—not just women—I hope you will consider objecting immediately and publicly. When you say nothing, you are implicitly approving of what's happening. I suspect other men will also have noticed the bad behavior but lack your courage to speak up. Your example represents a force for change. Progress blooms from our ability to be flexible and to evolve. To shift the culture, you guys must take action. Your intervention is incredibly powerful.

I once joined a company that harbored a sexual predator. Although we had proof of his terrible behavior, I believe we would not have been able to bring him down if several of his male subordinates had not been brave enough to step forward. It was not until they attested to a pattern of repugnant behavior that the company developed the backbone to act.

We've all learned from movies about school bullies that speaking up comes with a price. You might find yourself criticized for doing what you thought was the right thing, from either men or women or both! Don't take it too hard. You're still a hero in my eyes.

MY WONDER WOMAN FANTASY

A lot of women working in male-dominated industries are really lonely. I run a website with advice about how men and women can work together, and I can see what search terms have led someone to my site. Most of the search terms are related to male-dominated environments, such as "how to work with men," "women in mostly-male environment," "career advice for industry dominated by men," "tips for working in all-male office," and "navigating a male-dominated meeting."

Some of them are pretty sad. One poor woman googled "I'm the only woman in the office. Why won't they talk to me?" Another day, someone wrote, "I'm the only woman in a male-dominated office and they talk badly about me." That one made me mad. Thinking about the male behavior that would prompt this woman to seek help online about a vile office environment really ticked me off. I imagined the guys' malicious comments, hateful chuckles, and adolescent savagery, and steam started to come out of my ears. Then I had a brilliant idea.

I could use this information to take down some bad guys. I could become a woman of action instead of a mild-mannered writer. Rather than being endlessly frustrated by gender bias, I could take the fight to the office. Suppose I developed a Defense Against the Dark Snarks team. When a woman googled that kind of plea for help, I could track her IP address and gather my team outside her company's door to do a little gender schooling.

Some rational part of my brain pointed out that my little initiative might face some legal hurdles. I can only imagine what charges a creative attorney would file against me following such an assault. Instead maybe I could go for calling the bad guys out by blasting Phil Collins' "I Saw What You Did" outside their door. Or sending an embarrassing howler à la Harry Potter that flies around the office shrieking and scolding. Or leaving a card hanger on the door that says, "*Sorry we missed you. We'll be back—The Gender Equality Police.*" But, even then, there are likely to be some technical hurdles, as well as some privacy issues, if some women don't want me fighting their battles. Plus the National Security Agency wouldn't like me cutting in on its turf. After a few more rational thoughts, I sadly put my superhero fantasy aside.

So it's up to you guys. You're going to have to help her out. It would make a big difference to her if a guy were friendly and helpful without expecting sexual favors in return.

YOUR MOTIVATION

Men sometimes comment that they became more supportive of gender equality after they had daughters. They now mentor and advise women and support their advancement as they hope others will eventually do for their daughters. Me, I'll take what I can get—if a guy is helpful to his female co-workers, I don't question his motivation, but others aren't so generous. That's why you'll hear the battle cry: "Don't do it because you have daughters! Do it because she's a human being!" I don't agree, but I want you to be forewarned. In this climate, don't mention your personal relationships when you discuss your drive to create a better workplace. Just say you're trying to do the right thing.

And I'm sure you're shocked to hear that the world isn't rational and that not all women agree about how men should behave. Shocked.

YOUR OWN DILEMMA

I've made it sound pretty easy to build a better workplace, right? Listen, don't act like a jerk, stand up for women—you're doing great! Uh, not so fast. Helping women carries its own double-edged sword.

An article in *Men's Fitness* said that women find men who

stand up for someone more manly. Besides improving the world, that sounds like a good side benefit, right? Unfortunately not all women perceive it that way. If they think you're implying that women are weak creatures who need a man to look out for them, beware. You are at risk of being slapped down. You'll find that out the first time a woman says to you, "I don't need your help! I can take care of myself!" I'm going to be so sad to see the look on your face, but that's how some see it.

Navigating these waters will require a delicate touch. If you couch your actions in terms of what's fair and right, I think you'll be fine. If you make it sound like you're some valiant savior of women, you are asking for trouble.

HARD TIMES

Despite the plight of women in corporate America, many resent the suggestion that men should join in. We have become so enamored with the notions of "girl power," "the future is female," and "the best man for a job is a woman" that common sense has gone out the window. Painfully, when anyone proposes that men act on women's behalf, the conversation dissolves into a morass of defiance, victim blaming, male bashing, and all kinds of unpleasantries. What can I tell you? These topics are fraught right now with hysteria and polarization, and there are a lot of idiots out there. While I hope that your efforts will be recognized as those of a well-intentioned good guy, all bets are off. Whether that deters you or not is up to you. Me? I just keep at it. Each day I work on what's in front of me.

I'M ASKING

In my opinion, we do need help from men in straightening out our workplaces. Too many women are unhappy and mistreated at work, usually at the hands of men. We can't make progress without male cooperation. Men have a lot of power and smarts—it would be dumb not to ask them to join us. They can make things happen, and we haven't done very well without them. So, guys, would you jump on up in the front seat, please? It's a metaphorical seat, so there's lots of room. We need everyone for this fight.

A STARTING PLACE

There's always more to say about this complicated topic, but what you have read will get you started. As someone who has devoted considerable effort to improving gender relations, I am dismayed by the apparent worsening of the battle between the sexes over the past year. However, despite the large amount of ink that has been spilled, men and women still can work productively together, really enjoy each other's company, and develop collegial relationships that last a lifetime.

I hope this little book is useful and serves to improve work cultures. It will have served its purpose if *you* feel more comfortable interacting with women at work and more confident in your ability to build strong relationships with them. By caring for and learning from each other, perhaps we can view the other sex with tolerance, kindness, and—dare I say it—love.

Ending

Let's make this the beginning of the discussion. I'm interested in your experiences and feedback. You can find me through my website discreetguide.com. And good luck to you.

Join The Quest

It's time to fix bad work environments. Too many people are unhappy at their jobs because of mean bosses, flawed management, weak leadership, harassment, bullying, poor compensation, unfair promotion practices, conflicted HR staff, ambiguous goals, mediocre meetings, fuzzy reporting lines—the list goes on and on. Will you join me in spreading good management practices to create cultures that are welcoming to people of all colors, genders, sizes, ages, and perspectives? Diversity works best when everyone speaks and everyone listens. Let's do this!

If you would like to join my quest, you can sign up here: http://eepurl.com/dqLRjb

Author Biography

Jennifer K. Crittenden earned a BA in linguistics and French from Indiana University, a baccalaureate certificate in film studies, and an MBA in finance and MIS from the Kelley School of Business. She is a member of Phi Beta Kappa and received a CEL-TA diploma from the University of Cambridge to teach English as a second language.

For more than twenty years, she worked in corporate finance for big pharma and biotech companies in the US, UK, and Europe, rising from financial analyst to CFO.

She is the author of *The Discreet Guide for Executive Women: How to Work Well with Men (and Other Difficulties)*, an Amazon bestseller and winner of the 2012 National Independent Excellence Award in the Business-Motivational Category. In 2014, she published her second book, *You Not I: Exceptional Presence through the Eyes of Others*.

Jennifer offers professional development training programs through her company *The Discreet Guide®* on interpersonal, communication, performance, presentation, and language skills. She was also the executive coach for the Executive Presence program offered through the University of Wisconsin and MBA Women International. She writes and speaks frequently on topics related to gender, communication, and work.

Jennifer lived in Mammoth Lakes, California, for two years and wrote *The Mammoth Letters: Running Away to a Mountain Town*, which was published in 2017. She currently lives in San Diego, California, with her family.

Acknowledgments

First and foremost, I would like to thank the many men who advised and supported me during my corporate career. As managers, bosses, colleagues, contacts, friends, and acquaintances, they made my professional life rewarding and interesting. I am forever in your debt, guys. It was a lot of fun.

This book grew out of an article that I published on LinkedIn. I am grateful for the feedback and comments I received from people I knew and didn't know. Their input was very valuable. Readers of early drafts of the book also helped clarify my message and keep me honest. I appreciate their time and interest.

San Diego Women in Finance was kind enough to host a round table discussion to solicit advice from their members about working with women. The willingness of the attendees to share their experiences was very valuable.

Shannon Sorrells and Brenda Beckett provided expert review of the sections related to legal issues and human resources. The book benefited significantly from their input, and I am grateful for their enthusiasm and support.

Once again, my dear editor, Melanie Astaire Witt, took up the mantle as my partner in crime. Not only is she game, she's got skills. Her exquisite work shines on every page, but all errors are of my own making.

I also want to thank the members and associates of the Crittenden family, who continue to encourage my writing. And for their smart-alecky comments and insightful observations, my love goes to the Harvey boys, Tom, Luc, and Julian.

Other Resources

My website discreetguide.com has articles, jokes, book reviews, and past issues of *The Pergola*, a digital bimonthly magazine of information curated for the busy professional.

Articles or press releases on the website that were referenced in the book include:

A MAN Is Not an ATM

Beyond "You Look Nice"

Bullies at Large

The Discreet Guide Releases New Study Indicating Executive Presence Is Learned Rather than Inborn, with Both Genders Feeling Equally Confident (or Not) about Their Presence

Do You Have the Right Boss, Organizationally?

The F-Word (Or, Why Can't We All Just Get Along)

Gender Matters: Cases of Mistaken . . . Gender

The Hidden Risk of Business Travel: Scandal

Is Bullying the New Witch Hunt?

Newsflash from the Dropouts: We Have Not Forgotten

Quiz: Are You Cut Out to Work with Men?

Searching for Equality

Some Girls Are Better than Others

"Sorry Ladies"—The Dark Side of Workplace Humor

Threading the Needle—Advice for Women Working in a Male-Dominated Environment

Workplace Humor: Five Golden Rules

Recommended Books

Babcock, Linda, and Laschever, Sara. *Women Don't Ask: The High Cost of Avoiding Negotiation—and Positive Strategies for Change.* New York: Bantam Books, 2007.

Tannen, Deborah. *Talking from 9 to 5: Women and Men at Work.* New York: HarperCollins, 1994.

Valian, Virginia. *Why So Slow? The Advancement of Women.* Cambridge, MA: MIT Press, 1999.

Index

V

volume 30

W

woman-haters 104
women's groups 102
words to avoid 48

Y

You Don't Count 30